More Praise for *Leadership for a Fractured World*

"Drawing on deep experience advising presidents and founders of countries; executives in business, government, and nonprofits; teachers; and grassroots organizers, Dean Williams offers an enormously practical set of tools and insights for leading across boundaries in our divided yet interdependent world. The wisdom of this book is invaluable and lifesaving. Practical, inspiring, and rich with illuminating stories, this is essential reading for leadership today."
—**Ronald Heifetz, King Hussein bin Talal Senior Lecturer in Public Leadership, Harvard Kennedy School, and author of *Leadership without Easy Answers***

"*Leadership for a Fractured World* is not your typical leadership manual; it's an experience. It immediately drives you to want to act differently. Being part of a global organization and dealing with the need to constantly adapt to change makes one realize that creative leadership is necessary for coping with this complex environment. This book opens a world of possibilities that stay with you long after you finish reading it."
—**Limor Benderly, Leadership Continuity Director, Amdocs**

"Our world is shrinking. Civilizations once separated by oceans and continents now coexist in close proximity. We need leaders who can cross boundaries, build bridges, and lead change. Dean Williams has studied leaders all around the world. In this book, he shares his insights from his global learning experience. This is a must-read for all future leaders."
—**Kishore Mahbubani, former Singapore Ambassador to the United Nations; Dean, Lee Kuan Yew School of Public Policy, National University of Singapore; and author of *The Great Convergence***

"Dean Williams's new framework of leadership provides deep insight for situations where silos impede innovation. All businesses need this book!"
—**Takayoshi Yamakawa, President, Dream Incubator Inc., Japan**

"This is a great guide for those who want to understand the secret to leadership—and why we need dynamic leadership more than ever in this crazy, fractured world!"
—**Srdja Popovic, Executive Director, Centre for Applied Nonviolent Action and Strategies**

"This is a landmark book for those who are passionate about making a real difference in the world. Full of rich examples of leading change, it provides a no-nonsense approach to understanding and tackling the underlying fractures in organizations and communities. The book is a bridge builder in itself, spanning many disciplines and weaving a compelling narrative that will transform the way you think about leadership. It will stimulate and provoke the new conversations we urgently need to repair our fractured world."
—**Paul Porteous, Executive Director, Centre for Social Leadership, Australia**

"Williams does even more here than reflect on his decades of successful leadership as advisor and teacher. He also shows himself to be canny, generous, and self-reflexive in ways that make him an admirable model for his growing circle of purposeful readers. Williams links together a variety of lessons for *Leadership for a Fractured World*. As an architect of bridges over apparently impassable differences, Williams structures his multidimensional advice on pillars of every relevant discipline, including the arts and psychology, along with politics and economics. All of these he has studied with the open-mindedness and the humility that he recommends for aspiring leaders. A fractured world urgently needs the kind of passionate and principled leadership that Williams offers, sustained by moments for humor, the pleasures of collective art forms, and the deep satisfaction of cocreating new accords."

—Doris Sommer, Director, Cultural Agents Initiative, Harvard University

"Given the deeply held but often conflicting beliefs of people everywhere, this wonderful book is necessary reading for each of us attempting to navigate the complex realities confronting organizations and people today."

—David Chamberlain, Senior Vice President, M&T Bank, and CEO, Buffalo Promise Neighborhood

"A must-read for any leader! Our world is so globalized on the one hand and so divided by intolerance and tribalism on the other it needs leaders who are able to understand enigmatic problems, appreciate conflicting perspectives, and operate in complex environments. This book will help you become a global change agent by helping people transcend their differences and work together in the construction of a new world order."

—Jamil Mahuad, Mayor of Quito, 1992–1998, and President of Ecuador, 1998–2000

LEADERSHIP

—— for a ——

FRACTURED
WORLD

—— HOW TO ——
CROSS BOUNDARIES,
BUILD BRIDGES,
AND LEAD CHANGE

LEADERSHIP

—— *for a* ——

FRACTURED

WORLD

Dean Williams

BK

Berrett–Koehler Publishers, Inc.
a BK Business book

Berrett-Koehler Publishers, Inc.
1333 Broadway, Suite 1000
Oakland, CA 94612-1921
Tel: (510) 817-2277   Fax: (510) 817-2278   www.bkconnection.com

Ordering Information

Quantity sales. Special discounts are available on quantity purchases by corporations, associations, and others. For details, contact the "Special Sales Department" at the Berrett-Koehler address above.

Individual sales. Berrett-Koehler publications are available through most bookstores. They can also be ordered directly from Berrett-Koehler:
Tel: (800) 929-2929; Fax: (802) 864-7626; www.bkconnection.com

Orders for college textbook/course adoption use. Please contact Berrett-Koehler:
Tel: (800) 929-2929; Fax: (802) 864-7626.

Orders by U.S. trade bookstores and wholesalers. Please contact Ingram Publisher Services, Tel: (800) 509-4887; Fax: (800) 838-1149; E-mail: customer.service@ ingrampublisherservices.com; or visit www.ingrampublisherservices.com/Ordering for details about electronic ordering.

Berrett-Koehler and the BK logo are registered trademarks of Berrett-Koehler Publishers, Inc.

Printed in the United States of America

Berrett-Koehler books are printed on long-lasting acid-free paper. When it is available, we choose paper that has been manufactured by environmentally responsible processes. These may include using trees grown in sustainable forests, incorporating recycled paper, minimizing chlorine in bleaching, or recycling the energy produced at the paper mill.

Production Management: Michael Bass Associates
Cover Design: Kirk DouPonce

Library of Congress Cataloging-in-Publication Data
Williams, Dean, 1955–
    Leadership for a fractured world : how to cross boundaries, build bridges, and lead change / Dean Williams.
        pages   cm
    Includes bibliographical references and index.
    ISBN 978-1-62656-265-3 (pbk.)
    1. Leadership. I. Title.
HM1261.W548 2015
303.3'4—dc23
                                                                      2014041509
First Edition
20   19   18   17   16   15   10   9   8   7   6   5   4   3   2   1

To Rosie

To Mum

Contents

SEVEN   Expanding Your Personal Boundaries   165

EIGHT   Keeping Yourself from Fracturing   185

        Notes   207

        Acknowledgments   225

        Index   227

        About the Author   241

Foreword

By His Holiness The Dalai Lama

M any of the world's problems and conflicts arise because we have lost sight of the basic humanity that binds us all together as a human family. We tend to forget that despite the diversity of race, religion, ideology, and so forth, people are equal in their basic wish for peace and happiness.

When we see pictures of our blue planet from space, there are no signs of boundaries. It's a vivid illustration of the oneness of humanity. This is why we have to make the well-being of humanity our primary concern. We have efficient education and remarkable technological development, yet we still face many problems. None of us want these problems, but we seem to create them for ourselves. Why? Because we are too self-centered; we place too much stress on our own narrow interests with not enough consideration for the needs of others.

Today, despite ongoing conflicts and the threat of terrorism, most people are genuinely concerned about world peace, far less interested in propounding ideology, and far more committed to coexistence.

During the twentieth century, a greater number of human beings met their deaths through violence than at any other time, and the damage done to the natural environment was very serious. But as a result of these experiences, humanity is becoming more mature. This is evident in the growing concern for peace, nonviolence, and human rights. Even politicians increasingly talk about "'compassion'" and "'reconciliation.'" Despite a faltering start, the twenty-first century could become one of dialogue, one in which compassion, the seed of nonviolence, will be able to flourish.

We may sometimes feel that we can solve a problem quickly by force, but such success is often achieved at the expense of the rights and welfare of others. One problem may have been solved, but the seed of another is planted, thus opening a new chapter in a cycle of violence and counterviolence. Preventive measures and restraint have to be adopted right from the start. Clearly leaders need to be alert, far-sighted, and decisive. Mahatma Gandhi, who was such a leader, pointed out that, if we are seriously interested in peace, it must be achieved through peaceful and nonviolent means.

I believe that in ancient times the status of men and women was more or less equal, with everyone sharing an equal load of work. Then, with the establishment of settled communities, power became a factor between them. And the basis for power was physical; therefore, because they are generally physically stronger, men came to predominate. In modern times, with the introduction of education for all, the basis for power, survival, and improvement has been the brain, so the difference between men and women has changed and become less obvious. Now, when the world is so much more interdependent, compassion and warm-heartedness are required, and women have an equal responsibility to lead.

In today's reality, the only way of resolving differences is through dialogue and compromise, through human understanding and humility. We need to address the gap between rich and poor. Inequality, with some sections of humanity living in abundance while others on the same planet go hungry, is morally wrong and practically a source of problems. Equally important is the issue of freedom. As long as there is no freedom in some parts of the world, there can be no real peace and in a sense no real freedom for the rest of the world.

Perhaps the most important factors that inhibit us are short-sightedness, narrow-mindedness, and selfishness. The challenge for leaders is to help people transcend self-interest and the immediate interests of their group in order to collaborate and promote shared happiness.

I hope and pray that readers of this book by Dean Williams will contribute to the good of the world by taking the initiative in giving a lead wherever they can to help our communities and societies solve the toughest problems. Peaceful living is about trusting those on whom we depend and caring for those who depend on us. If even a few individuals create mental peace and happiness within themselves and act responsibly and kind-heartedly toward others, they will have a positive influence in their community. Our goal should be a more peaceful and equitable world, not only for the present generation, but also for our children and the generations to come.

Preface

This book is about helping people and groups that have great differences come together to solve shared problems. It is about providing leadership to address the interdependent challenges, real dangers, and abundant opportunities generated by the fractured, complex, and unpredictable world in which we live. Interdependent problems cannot be resolved by one group acting alone or in isolation, and therefore a new notion of leadership and change is needed. Today we need to be global change agents.

By "global change agent," I do not mean someone crisscrossing the globe solving world problems but anyone, at the local or international level, who has a broad mindset and is committed to making the world a better place. The global change agent (1) mobilizes people to cross the boundaries that divide groups to address shared problems; (2) helps groups bust the boundaries and maladaptive practices that keep people from effectively responding to emerging threats and the demands of a changing world; (3) works with divided and fractured groups to build a relational bridge by healing wounds, reducing the mystery of the other, and resolving conflicts; and (4) intervenes when a group is stuck to stimulate sufficient creativity to transcend confining boundaries to produce breakthrough solutions.

Global change agents who can exercise leadership are needed at all levels of society and in all domains of human activity. The book is for leaders in business, politics, nongovernmental organizations (NGOs), international organizations, education, and government. It is for anyone who must work across silos, divisions, and borders to exercise leadership. It is for those with considerable power who seek to lead from positions of authority and for those with little power who seek to lead from the margins or at the grassroots. Fundamentally, the book is for those passionate and committed people who desire to contribute to a better world. The reality is that, in so many areas, our world is fractured, and small fault lines and deep chasms divide groups. There is much work to be done at both the local and international levels to fix what is broken, pursue value-adding opportunities, and help groups transcend their differences to create something of worth for all.

The ideas and principles presented in this book have been shaped by conversations I have had with many leaders and change agents. At the Harvard Kennedy School, I chair The Global Change Agent executive education program, and I have been enriched by the experiences and insights of the participants. I also direct the World Leaders Project, based at the Center for Public Leadership, and have had the special opportunity to interview many leaders to get their advice and lessons. These include Gordon Brown of the United Kingdom, Lee Kuan Yew of Singapore, Mary Robinson of Ireland and the United Nations, Shimon Peres of Israel, Malcolm Fraser of Australia, Felipe Calderón of Mexico, Lech Walesa of Poland, and the Dalai Lama, to name just a few. I have also interviewed many change agents in business, public service, education, NGOs, and civil society. These are people at the forefront of change, whether as activists, organizers, educators, entrepreneurs, managers, thinkers, or innovators.

The book also draws on my experience helping groups change. I have worked with many corporations on leadership development and cultural change to help them become more adaptive and globally competitive. I have participated in large-scale change initiatives in educational reform in Australia and the United States. I have also been an adviser to many different governments, including Nigeria, Brunei, and East Timor. For several years, I served as the chief adviser to the president of Madagascar, helping him facilitate the development of one of the poorest nations on the planet. Significant progress was being made until a rogue faction in the military launched an ugly coup in 2009.

When it comes to leadership and change, I have seen the good, the bad, and the ugly. This book captures my insights.

Leadership for a fractured world is a complex topic, and no single theory can do it justice. Therefore, I have adopted a multidisciplinary approach in the writing of this book by drawing on research and theories from anthropology, social psychology, human development, and business.

The book is also a contribution to the adaptive leadership framework, as first articulated by Ronald Heifetz and Riley Sinder in their seminal paper that distinguished leadership from authority, and technical work from adaptive work.[1] Both are my friends, colleagues, and collaborators, and we continue to work together to push the frontier of the understanding and teaching of adaptive leadership.

How should you use this book? I have not written it with the intention of giving clear-cut prescriptive answers, as one might do in writing about performance management where the problem and goals are clear. This is a book about addressing messy, adaptive problems that have no clear textbook answers. I present guidelines, ideas, and cases that illustrate ways to think about how to approach these kinds of problems. By describing an array of cases of men and women succeeding or failing in a variety of contexts, I hope that you, the reader, will draw connections to your own particular leadership challenges. Think about what the boundaries are that confine or limit you, your group, or organization. Think about the boundaries that need to be crossed, busted, or transcended. Think about the kind of leadership you need to provide to make the world a better place. I hope the principles presented will help you on your leadership journey.

INTRODUCTION

It's a Crazy,
Fractured World

*There is nothing more difficult to take in hand, more perilous
to conduct, or more uncertain in its success, than to take
the lead in the introduction of a new order of things.*
NICCOLÒ MACHIAVELLI (1469–1527)

I t's a crazy world, and it is a fractured world, and we all feel
the stress and see the fractures, and frustratingly ask, "Where
is the leadership?" I have been wrestling with this question
for a long time.

As a young doctoral student, I lived for a time in the remote
rainforests of Borneo with a nomadic tribe called the Penan, where
I studied social and cultural adaptation. The Penan hunted with a
blowpipe, wore a simple loincloth, and had boar tusks protruding
through their pierced earlobes. One evening eating sago palm and
roasted monkey around the campfire and telling stories, a small
group of Penan young men arrived after having spent a month
away working for a logging company. They brought with them a
"boom box," and I shall never forget when they turned it on and
Madonna's voice could be heard screeching through the forest,
"Like a virgin, touched for the very first time. . . ." As she sang,

I thought, "This is surreal—and depressing—as the Penan's life will never be the same."

The intrusive aspects of globalization had disrupted the Penan's life and also disrupted one of the world's most magnificent and essential rainforests—and not just because of Madonna's singing, but because of the competition of diverse groups for scarce and valuable resources. The developed nations of the world wanted the hardwoods in the Penan's forest for the building of houses and furniture, the government wanted the revenues from deforestation for development, and entrepreneurial businessmen and some politicians saw an unprecedented opportunity to make a quick profit. Saving the forest and ensuring the Penan had a say in their future was a complex challenge involving many groups with competing priorities and values: the local government, environmental activists, the World Bank, the nations that purchased the timber, and, of course, the Penan themselves.

The reality is that even though media technology is breaking down boundaries and connecting us in unprecedented ways, fractures are abundant and all groups are in a state of volatility and vulnerability—whether it is the Penan of Borneo or an investment bank on Wall Street.

Today we need men and women who have the courage and the capacity to orchestrate multidimensional problem solving and change to address complex challenges. This is a different kind of leadership than what we have become accustomed to. Traditional forms of leadership, in particular what I call "big man leadership," tend to advance the interests of one group over another and inadvertently perpetuate fractures and divisions.

Fractures and divisions are reinforced by group boundaries. Boundaries could be professional, structural, cultural, ideological, ethnic, gender, or religious boundaries, to name just a few. They create and protect spaces within which coordinated work and living processes take place. A boundary is a form of constraint, but it is also a frontier. As a frontier it presents fascinating opportunities for exploration, learning, expansion, and creative discovery. To mobilize people to address interdependent challenges and to orchestrate change, leaders work at the boundaries. While traditional leaders reinforce boundaries, change agents exercise leadership to help groups expand boundaries, cross divides, and build bridges to address shared challenges.

If groups and institutions do not have enough people providing leadership to address fractures and to mobilize people to tackle interdependent problems, they will fail to deliver on their promise, persist in a state of mediocrity, and might even collapse. They will certainly not be as productive as they could be.

For example, a multinational software company that I advise is struggling with the challenge of being a truly global company. It has more than ten thousand employees in different parts of the world. The dilemma is that internal silos inhibit the communication, coordination, and problem solving needed to take the company to the next level of performance, innovation, and profitability. Many of the executives, by inclination or preference, stay within their group enclave, get stuck or lost in hierarchy and procedure, and do not display the initiative needed to cross boundaries and build the relationships needed to produce innovative breakthroughs for the company. A senior human resources executive who saw this pattern as a high-priority challenge asked me, "How can we shake these people out of their comfort zones and get them to be global leaders of change?"

Companies are not alone in this challenge. Educational systems, governments, and every group or tribe in the world today face the challenge of dealing with complexity, interdependence, inhibiting boundaries, and the demands for change. Whether you are the police chief in Ferguson, Missouri; a community activist in Bogotá, Colombia; a school principal in Geelong, Australia; the mayor of Beijing; the head of an NGO in Liberia; a software engineer in Silicon Valley; or a businessman in Tokyo, you must learn how to provide change agent leadership to address the array of complex problems and challenges facing your particular group, organization, or community.

Chapter 1 of this book talks about why the world is a crazy and fractured place. It explains how the cultural drift of groups—the habitual ways of thinking and operating—thwarts problem solving and creative work as it pertains to addressing interdependent challenges. The chapter explains why big man leadership—the expression of prominence, dominance, and tribalizing—is insufficient for dealing with complex problems, and why global change agents are needed.

Chapter 2 addresses the diagnostic work needed to figure out where the fractures are and why they persist. It explores how cultural practices, sacred values, and group narratives generate divisions between groups, reinforce group boundaries, and impede interdependent problem solving. The chapter presents a diagnostic framework for analyzing group dynamics and determining both the adaptive and maladaptive features of group behavior. Maladaptive group features will need to be modified, while adaptive features can be leveraged to support the work of problem solving and change.

Chapter 3 presents the specific leadership challenge of crossing boundaries. To provide leadership, you must cross multiple boundaries to mobilize diverse groups to tackle interdependent problems. Crossing boundaries is not easy or natural. It can also be risky because you must leave a state of predictability and safety for a state of vulnerability and uncertainty. You need to be responsible for what blessing or threat you represent to diverse groups and find wise partners to help navigate the terrain and deal with boundary keepers if you are to succeed in your leadership efforts.

Chapter 4 explains the leadership challenge of busting boundaries. Boundaries are reinforced by group values, habits, and practices. They can be like walls that limit people's capacity to see and respond to the realities of changing conditions, new threats, and exciting opportunities. Group members might not consider the boundary as a constraint but as a welcome protective barrier that allows them to continue doing what they always have done. The task of the change agent is to challenge one's own group's boundaries, help people appreciate what is at stake if they do not change, and work with them to eliminate those practices that reduce their capacity to connect, adapt, and succeed.

Chapter 5 presents the leadership challenge of transcending boundaries. Transcending boundaries is creative work. It is about helping the group depart from the familiar and venture into unfamiliar terrain with a spirit of exploration, experimentation, and discovery. It includes harnessing the power of diversity to engage in innovation to generate novel and breakthrough solutions.

Chapter 6 presents the leadership challenge of building a bridge between groups. Enmity, or the fact that different groups are simply a mystery to one another, may cause or perpetuate a deep divide between groups. Wounds must be healed, the mystery must be reduced, relationships must be rebuilt, and collaborative work on behalf of a shared future must begin.

Chapter 7 explains how to expand your personal boundaries in order to increase your capacity to provide leadership for a crazy and fractured world. Leadership requires getting others to expand, bust, and transcend boundaries, but if you cannot do likewise, how can you lead? Expanding personal boundaries is about broadening your mindset to become more globally oriented, developing in cultural and moral wisdom, and enhancing your capacity to operate in complex, chaotic, and diverse environments.

Chapter 8, the final chapter, speaks to how to keep oneself from fracturing or succumbing to the strain of leading in a crazy world. In exercising leadership as a global change agent, it is easy to get tired, become cynical, burn out, or give up. The burden of responsibility, as well as the risk and danger, cannot be taken out of the work, but you can increase your capacity, effectiveness, and resilience in the face of these demands. Your personal challenge is not only to survive but to thrive, and to find joy and satisfaction in this noble work of making the world a better place.

PART 1

Preparation

CHAPTER 1

What Leadership for a Fractured World Entails

The world in so many ways is fractured. The fractures in groups and between groups could be wide fractures that divide, hairline fractures that generate a state of susceptibility and vulnerability, or latent fault lines that can crack open when some sudden change erupts due to internal or external pressure. Many groups, institutions, and communities are in a fractured state in varying degrees. Somehow, we seem to hobble along, but the reality is few things quite live up to their promise. In fact, what we repeatedly see are systems breaking down—be they institutional systems, economic systems, political systems, or environmental systems, to name but a few—and we all frustratingly ask, "Where is the leadership?"

To provide leadership for a fractured world, we need a different way to think about leadership. We cannot think of leadership exclusively in terms of the "big man" or the "tribal boss" who represents the interests of their group alone. We need to distinguish real leadership from formal authority.[1] Leaders today must be agents of change who are willing and able to cross boundaries, connect groups, and orchestrate multidimensional problem solving and change. Without that kind of leadership, the fractures that separate us will only get worse.

Leadership Is Needed to Help Groups Transcend the Tribal Impulse to Solve Interdependent Problems

Most people do not fully appreciate the systemic nature of their problems. We think and act parochially. The cultures of our respective groups and the respective roles we play in these groups often cause us to view problems through the narrow and myopic lens of immediate self- or group interest. Consequently, groups are inclined to see only pieces of a complex problem and end up working on their own small bit without making much headway.

Even though we live in a globalized world, in many ways we are still very tribal. By "tribal," I mean that we affiliate ourselves with groups that inform our identity and from which we derive meaning. These days, many of us belong to multiple tribes—the company tribe, the church tribe, the family tribe, and even many online tribes. Tribal groups since the beginning of time have been important for community and security. When a group gets too big or amorphous, it is easy to get lost and feel uneasy, so for biological, psychological, and cultural reasons we retreat to the safety of some form of an identity group or tribe.

Social science research on group behavior supports the notion of tribalism and explains how it generates in-groups and out-groups. The renowned Harvard biologist and naturalist, E. O. Wilson, has articulated the tribal impulse by arguing that as human beings, we have innate tendencies, predispositions, and emotional capacities that lead us to identify with a group—or tribe—that provides fellowship, protection, coordinating mechanisms, parameters for action, and frameworks for interpreting the human experience.[2] While tribal by nature, we are willing to create networks of tribes to expand boundaries, colonize territory, engage in trade and agriculture, and go to war and defeat enemies. In his insightful book *Moral Tribes*, Joshua Greene, who directs the Moral Cognition Lab at Harvard, describes how our brains are designed for tribal life, leading us to make choices to advance our own group's interests at the expense of others and to rationalize such behavior as appropriate and moral.[3] The tribal impulse indicates that we want to be around people who are similar to us in terms of values, looks, language, humor, food, and desires.

The tribal impulse can be seen even in progressive places such as Belgium, the nation whose capital houses the headquarters for the European Union. The EU offices in Brussels may symbolize unity, yet all is not well in Belgium. Some Dutch-speaking people of the Flanders region want to separate from the French-speaking people of the Walloon region. Their tensions are rooted in historical, economic, cultural, linguistic, and political differences. Rather than do the hard work of learning from one another and maintaining a viable and thriving nation, too many people would prefer to call it a day and retreat to what they believe to be the safe confines of their tribal identity.[4]

The tribal impulse is evident in commercial enterprises, too, as it pertains to professions and departments. Conducting research at a major American newspaper, I noticed how the suspicions between the journalists and editors on one side and the business managers and marketing people on the other side kept the two groups from talking to one another. In fact, they worked on different floors to avoid interaction. What surprised me was the intensity of the contempt each group had for the other. The journalists detested the fact the business people made decisions based on market demographics and advertising revenues. The business people deplored how ignorant or naïve journalists could be about the realities of running a company that had to make money in order to survive.

Being tribally oriented is not a bad thing; in fact, it has many benefits. The problem, however, is that many of the challenges that we face today cannot be resolved if we think parochially and act tribally.

The tribal impulse is reinforced by group boundaries. These boundaries make addressing systemic, interdependent challenges very difficult. There are many kinds of boundaries, including religious, cultural, professional, geographic, economic, class, and ethnic boundaries. Every group has a boundary. Nature has boundaries, and all organisms have boundaries. The boundary protects the space that allows group activity to take place. If a boundary is absent or too permeable, the group or organism is weakened and could die or simply disappear.

While boundaries are essential for distinguishing group member-ship and for coordinating domains of group activity, their function is to keep some people in and others out. They work well in helping groups engage in routine problem solving, but they can be constrain-ing and burdensome when dealing with interdependent problems. Complexity does not honor boundaries but transcends them, as with a global financial crisis, a virus such as Ebola, sectarian warfare, or environmental pollution. If people are unwilling to transcend their boundaries and address an interdependent problem, they put at risk not only their group but the entire system.

Recently I met with some managers from one of the world's leading multinational software companies who were struggling to deal with a complicated challenge where a division overseas was having difficulty in getting its perspectives heard in the headquarters. By virtue of the reluctance to open the boundary and let the "foreign" perspective be included in the problem-solving and strategy-formulating processes of headquarters, vital data were not being considered, which in turn had an impact on overall company performance. This is a problem every large company struggles with. Boundaries that inhibit performance develop easily.

Managers in such environments can become excessively parochial, operating mostly within their boundaries and seeing no reason to cross boundaries, bust boundaries, or join with others to address a shared challenge. In boundary-laden organizations, silos begin to emerge that become rigid barriers to success. These silos lead people to engage in protective games, petty politics, and turf battles, which are activities that add no value to the organization but actually diminish value.

Globalization is breaking down many boundaries, yet many old fractures persist and new fractures are being generated. Former U.K. prime minister Gordon Brown stated that "globalization has generated opposite gravitational poles of production and consumption, and today the world arrangements look unbalanced and unsustainable." He added that while there are benefits to globalization, "they cannot be secured without a willingness to address, at a global level, the underlying economic, democratic, social and political weaknesses of globalization."[5] In other words, the problems generated by globalization are complex, interdependent, and systemic in nature and cannot be resolved by thinking parochially or acting tribally. Before the global financial crisis of 2008, Brown saw the need to get financial regulators to work together at a global level to understand the true scale of risk and act on it by creating an early-warning system. "I will forever regret my failure to bring other countries on board or persuade them of the urgency of action," he lamented. "I can see with hindsight . . . that it was impossible to build an international consensus."[6]

Leadership Is Needed to Help Groups Generate Shared Progress

While the tribal impulse is natural and brings many benefits, problems arise when groups pursue their goals without concern for the interests of other groups due to very different and often competing notions of progress.

Progress, according to the dictionary, means a move toward a "higher or better state." Any human organizational, social, political, or economic system will contain differences of opinion about what is meant by "higher" or "better" and the pathway for producing progress. For example, the prevailing belief among some groups is that democracy is the essential engine to generate progress throughout the world. But, as we have seen in Iraq and Afghanistan, American-style democracy cannot succeed without deep learning work to modify the values, perceptions, and priorities of multiple groups. And there are some groups that believe that progress can only be achieved by coercively getting other groups to abide by their beliefs, and should they refuse they need to be eradicated, as we have witnessed with radical religious groups in Iraq and Syria. In the context of the United States, the Republicans have one view of progress and the Democrats have another view, and within each of these groups are subfactions with their own particular beliefs about what progress is and how to generate it.

Healthy debate and the exchange of perspectives is a good thing, but when groups demand that their view of progress is the right one and the view of other factions is flawed or outright wrong, then the divisions make shared problem solving impossible. In 2013, for example, the fractured political culture in Washington led to a government shutdown when Congress failed to enact legislation to appropriate funds for the fiscal year.

People's definitions of progress are informed by their cultural heritage, group values, and personal aspirations. It is not enough to say that "we all want the same thing." We do not all want the same thing. As the previous examples indicate, even if our notions of progress are similar, the strategies and actions for producing progress may differ radically.

A leadership challenge is to keep groups from defining progress in narrow, parochial terms such as winning or beating the competition, and to view progress as making things sustainably better for all. In the context of an interdependent world, if you are attaining your goal through destructive competition, then instead of getting practical results, you might be setting the conditions for ongoing conflict and great loss—to your own group and to others.

Leadership Is Needed to Fix a Maladaptive Cultural Drift

Sometimes the impediment to progress lies in the deficient problem-solving processes embedded in the cultural drift of groups. All tribes, groups, and institutions have what I call a "cultural drift." The cultural drift is the group's shared, taken-for-granted values, practices, and priorities. It is the habitual way of operating. Members of the group essentially drift along in its cultural river, without thinking deeply about the implications of their actions and choices, because the cultural drift provides a set of processes and procedures for solving routine problems and addressing predictable challenges. This patterned behavior might work well in some contexts but be ineffective in others. Unless the group can modify its cultural drift to address complex, interdependent problems, a breakdown in the system could occur.

To illustrate the power of the drift in shaping and constraining action, consider what happened when an earthquake and tsunami struck the east coast of Japan on March 11, 2011, leading also to a nuclear disaster at the Fukushima nuclear power plant. After the tsunami hit the plant, a meltdown occurred at three of the six nuclear reactors, releasing substantial amounts of radioactive materials into the environment, and causing a mass evacuation of two hundred thousand people. An analysis by an independent commission concluded that while the tsunami triggered the event, it was also a man-made disaster that was the product of cultural, managerial, and regulatory deficiencies in the company, in the government, and between agencies. The chairman of the committee, Kiyoshi Kurokawa, stated:

> What this report cannot fully convey—especially to a global audience—is the mindset that supported the negligence behind this disaster. What must be admitted—very painfully—is that this was a disaster *Made in Japan*. Its fundamental causes are to be found in the ingrained conventions of Japanese culture: our reflexive obedience; our reluctance to question authority; our devotion to "sticking with the program"; our groupism; and our insularity.[7]

Chairman Kurokawa was particularly critical of the company that owned and ran the power plant, TEPCO. The report highlighted that management had a "disregard for global trends and a disregard for public safety," and the company was a business that "prioritized benefits to the organization at the expense of the public."[8] His report was also tough on the government, pointing out that the breakdown was made worse because the agency responsible for promoting nuclear power was also the agency charged with regulating the industry. The conflict in interest resulted in the lack of best-practice procedures and protocols needed to maximize safeguards and minimize the possibility of a disaster.

The report also drew attention to the fact that Japan's democratic processes were deficient in that the people's dissenting voices were not heard in a robust public discussion. Greater community participation and a strong civil society might have served as a watchdog to cast light on the flaws in government, industry, and prevailing cultural problem-solving practices pertaining to nuclear energy. But Japanese political authorities have never encouraged or valued groups agitating from the sidelines or raising potentially embarrassing or threatening questions. The report illustrates that the cultural drift that had served the country and its institutions well for generations—and still does for many challenges—had some maladaptive features that exacerbated the calamity.

Japan and TEPCO are not unusual. Authority figures in all groups, institutions, and cultures generally protect and promote the prevailing cultural drift as it pertains to problem solving and decision making, even if it has maladaptive features.

Groups, governments, and companies need adaptive and responsive cultural drifts. Given that it is a high-velocity world with extraordinary opportunities suddenly appearing and just as quickly disappearing, groups must be able to respond with speed and precision. For corporations, it is the age of hypercompetition. The abundance of new knowledge and technologies generates rich possibilities, yet human nature, the fractures that divide us, and the flawed features of the cultural drift of institutions make it difficult to capitalize on these advances to produce advantage for all.

There Is Too Much Prominence, Dominance, and Tribalizing—and Too Little Leadership

Where is the leadership to address the problems of a fractured world? What is leadership? If a Martian were to say, "Take me to your leader!" most people would probably take them to the dominant authority figure of a group, organization, or community. They would not necessarily take them to the provocative change agent who may have little status but is courageously crossing boundaries, asking tough questions, and seeking to mobilize diverse groups to face reality and tackle messy, shared problems that endanger a group or community. They would think the direction-setting, charismatic harmonizer who gets everyone marching in the same direction is the leader.

Indeed, most people generally think of the traditional, strong, boundary-reinforcing boss as the leader. It might be an expression of leadership, but it is what I term *big man leadership*, and it has both strengths and weaknesses. At its essence, big man leadership is about power, position, and formal authority. The conventional notion of leadership in most institutions and societies places the burden of direction setting, problem solving, and decision making on a dominant individual or elite group. The so-called leader is expected to show the way forward, protect the group, maintain group boundaries, and solve problems with minimal disruption to people's lives. His or her role is to be a symbol of the group's ideals and to act in ways that advance the group's interests, even if it is at the expense of other groups or the broader system. For many problems, big man leadership and the expression of formal authority is adequate to drive disparate groups to focus on the right set of tasks to achieve shared objectives. Today, however, power is dispersed and the world is too complex to rely exclusively on big man leadership. Leadership depth and breadth is needed.

The default strategy of big man leadership as it pertains to dealing with problems is generally through the expression of *prominence* ("Look to me—I'll fix the problem"), *dominance* ("Listen to me—Do what I say"), and *tribalizing* ("Follow me—I'll advance your interests"). Libya's Muammar Gaddafi is an extreme example, but the essence of his behavior illustrates the way many big man leaders operate as they go about the work of problem solving and change.

I once sat next to Colonel Gaddafi and his team for three days at an African Union meeting in Ghana. He was a surreal character in his extravagant flowing robes. When Gaddafi stood to address his fellow African heads of state, he received a standing ovation—for different reasons. One was the novelty factor. He looked unique and his flamboyant style of dress was a bold statement of grandiosity, sending a signal that he considered himself a force to be reckoned with. He was also seen as someone who stood up to the West and took a stand for Africa. Then he started speaking. While every other head of state spoke only for the allocated fifteen minutes, Gaddafi spoke for an hour. By the end of his speech, which was a rambling and erratic soliloquy on the threats of neo-imperialism and the need for Africa to be united in order to fight its Western opponents, most people were bored, chatting, or asleep. Even with his glorious outfit he could not hold their attention, and polite but weak applause was given as he concluded. What began with a bang ended with a fizzle.

Gaddafi was trying to be the agent of change by convincing his fellow African leaders that they should create a united Africa, something like the European Union or the United States. He failed because he did not understand that most Africans were resonating to different priorities than his. Gaddafi was still acting as the revolutionary zealot, while other leaders had practical concerns pertaining to building healthy economies and regional networks that would lift their people out of poverty by promoting trade relations for global competitiveness.

On October 20, 2011, three years after the Ghana speech, Gaddafi was killed by his own people. He was a tragic character who had the potential and resources to do great things in his own country and the region. His grandiose delusions and political ineptness, however, led him to pursue strategies that did little to generate the transformations that he publicly espoused. Instead, his actions perpetuated the divisions that had already existed while generating new ones.

It is not just wild dictators that provide big man leadership. Talented managers in all institutions can be guilty of such behavior. Their approach might succeed in generating results in a relatively stable and bounded environment, but when confronted with a novel or complex challenge their approach might manifest serious deficiencies. Consider the case of Lehman Brothers.

Lehman Brothers, one of the world's largest and oldest investment banks, collapsed in 2007 because of flaws in its corporate strategy and notions of leadership. Even as the U.S. housing market was faltering, CEO Richard Fuld pursued a highly aggressive, leveraged business model, putting the firm at even greater risk. Unlike some competitors that had had the foresight to sense the pending collapse and make a midcourse correction, Fuld refused to rethink his strategy or listen to those inside and outside the company who raised serious questions. He was too confident in his own answers—after all, he had been relatively successful at

Lehman Brothers for eighteen years. When he realized how bad the situation was, rather than be entirely truthful with investors, he presented an upbeat message regarding the company's strategy and financial well-being. Had he put reality in front of his management team and investors early enough, solutions might have been generated that saved the company.[9]

Before the collapse of Lehman Brothers, Richard Fuld explained his ideas on leadership to the students at the Wharton Business School.[10] His first principle was that "leaders earn the right to lead because they know more than others." His second principle was to "build a strong team around you" by promoting collaboration and harmony and discouraging conflict and open disagreement. "What I need," he said, "is peace in the family." His third principle was to "pick a strategy and stick with it." I suggest that Fuld's leadership principles contributed to the collapse of Lehman Brothers. His leadership challenge was to create the conditions that allowed, even encouraged, people to question the prevailing strategy when they anticipated danger, even if it generated internal conflict. Fuld was a talented big man leader, but his leadership was insufficient to save his company from collapse.

Big man leadership is really about authority, formal or informal. It is about one individual managing the group boundaries, showing the way forward, and articulating what is appropriate and inappropriate behavior. It can be expressed though benevolence and paternalism, and it can also be expressed through the aggressive assertion of power. Either way, there are limitations to what can be accomplished by relying exclusively on formal authority or prominence, dominance, and tribalizing.

Prominence is about status, and by virtue of having status, the group looks to you. Prominence leads to enormous burdens being placed on select individuals to be the problem solvers and experts.

Certainly expertise in a particular domain of knowledge can give you status and prominence, but experts acting alone cannot solve today's problems. Expertise is about depth of knowledge, but complex problems span boundaries and require diverse perspectives and integrated sources of knowledge. All individuals, no matter how prominent or talented they might be, are subject to error, and there can be dire consequences when they act alone, get it wrong, or fail to mobilize different perspectives to be included in the problem-solving process. For example, during a congressional hearing on the financial crisis of 2008, Congressman Henry Waxman asked the former head of the U.S. Federal Reserve, Alan Greenspan, "Do you feel that your ideology pushed you to make decisions that you wish you had not made?"[11] Greenspan conceded, "Yes, I've found a flaw. . . . I've been very distressed by that fact."[12] Greenspan thought that the free market would generate its own corrective mechanism and cause banks to take responsible action to fix flawed strategies before things got out of hand. Such was not the case. Fifteen banks collapsed in 2008, others were bailed out, and on one day alone, more than $1.2 trillion vanished from the U.S. stock market.[13]

We all have flaws in our reasoning and blind spots in our understanding that make it difficult to consistently provide successful leadership; therefore, on some challenges, it is easy for anyone to unwittingly become the source of counterfeit leadership—whether you are the chairman of the Federal Reserve, the manager of a nuclear power plant in Japan, the head of an NGO in Madagascar, or the CEO of a Wall Street investment bank with an MBA from Harvard.

Dominance is different from prominence. Prominence emphasizes "look to me, because I am the expert," while dominance emphasizes "listen to me, because I am the boss" Dominance is the expression of power and a form of control to get people to "do it my way." We see it expressed by the alpha chimp in chimpanzee communities, and we see it in human communities. Dominance is not necessarily negative as it does play an important role in maintaining order for a group and also in orienting people during times of distress. Any parent can attest to the need for displays of dominance from time to time, not that it always works. Dominance becomes problematic when it tries to solve problems for which the tools of command and control do not apply. To get people to face interdependent challenges, the exercise of leadership requires stimulating imagination and creativity, and the promotion of learning. Dominance is often used to suppress multiple perspectives, thwart creativity, and demand compliance—all in the name of maintaining the prevailing order and ensuring predictability and stability.

Tribalizing is the advancement of your group's interests at the expense of other groups. It is a very primal dynamic that leads a group to bestow authority on someone to fight their battles, protect their well-being, and be the gatekeeper of the group's boundaries. But oftentimes, if a group is to make progress by dealing with threats and taking advantage of new opportunities, the group must change some cherished values and practices. For many groups, protecting tribal interests and practices becomes more important than facing reality and addressing interdependent problems that can make life better for all groups.

Creating or perpetuating fractures often occurs through the words and actions of tribalizing authority figures and big man leaders. Fracturing actions give preference to your own group over another and trivialize, marginalize, or harm another group.

Fracturing words include disparaging comments about other groups, and speeches that appeal to your own group's narcissism and sense of superiority. Fracturing speech is divisive and exclusive, rather than uniting and inclusive. It perpetuates the myth that "We are good and the other is bad." It exploits the group's noble traditions and cultural pride to promote a sense of preeminence or uniqueness. It assigns all the bad stuff to an outside group and the good stuff to one's own group, and thereby allows people to avoid dealing with their own group's deficiencies and maladaptive values.

Fracturing tribalizing dynamics are common in politics. For example, the outspoken rock star Ted Nugent threw his celebrity weight behind a Republican candidate in Texas and, during an interview in 2014, he called President Obama a "subhuman mongrel." Not only were his comments fracturing, but they were offensive—not just to the president but to most Americans. Many members of the Republican Party quickly condemned Nugent's comments, but one powerful voice in the party, a former presidential candidate and media personality, Newt Gingrich, was glib. When pushed on the subject in a CNN interview, he agreed that what Nugent said was stupid, but he added to the fracture by turning it into a political fight, arguing that it was the Hollywood types and liberal media that were making all the fuss and that they had double standards.[14] Gingrich missed a unique opportunity to do important bridge-building leadership work and in that moment acted in ways that trivialized others' concerns. He might have intervened to promote the debate on media bias at another time and used that special moment on CNN, where he had the attention of the entire country, to do some important work around race and tolerance, particularly at a time when people felt that political fractures and social tensions were harming the country.

Given the Problems We Face, Leaders Must Cross Boundaries, Build Bridges, and Lead Change

To provide leadership for a fractured world, leaders must be change agents, even global change agents. Even if you are exercising leadership at the local level in an NGO, a school, or a company, you need a global orientation to appreciate how global or systemic forces impact what is happening at the local level that generate the demand for change. You need to appreciate both the strengths and constraining aspects of culture and, when the problem calls for it, transcend cultural constraints and group boundaries to mobilize diverse factions to tackle shared problems.

Change agents are attention managers—they intervene to get and keep the spotlight on interdependent problems. Big man leaders put the spotlight on themselves. They use prominence and dominance to get the group to follow them, because they believe that they know what needs to be done. As attention managers, change agents want people to see the systemic nature of the challenge and appreciate what progress is at risk if it is not actively addressed. They are interested not in getting people to follow them but in getting people to face the complexity of the problem.

The rock star Bono exercised leadership as a change agent by getting President George Bush's secretary of the treasury, Paul O'Neill, to visit Africa with him and call attention to issues of HIV, rampant poverty, educational deficiencies, and disease. The two were branded the "odd couple" because they were diametrically opposites in style, politics, and professions. But for two weeks they conversed, debated, shared stories, and explored options for addressing some of the most intractable problems.[15] The creative partnership of Bono and O'Neill served—for a moment, at least—to get many people thinking about Africa and the plight of the poor, the sick, and the disenfranchised. It put the spotlight on issues that many people in the developed world prefer to ignore. One reporter noted that Bono "opened up new frontiers . . . by leaving the protestors of Seattle and Genoa behind him for the deep corridors of power, in particular the White House. The argument is that real change comes from influencing those in power, not throwing stones at them."[16]

Many interdependent problems are adaptive problems. In our leadership classes at Harvard, my colleagues and I teach students to distinguish between adaptive and technical problems. Technical problems are clear-cut problems. The application of expertise or the accumulated knowledge of the group is generally sufficient to reach resolution. Even if the technical challenge is complicated, if you get enough smart people to address the problem and provide them with sufficient time and resources, they can fix it. Moreover, technical problems can often be solved within the current structures of an organization that are designed to process them with efficiency and routine. In contrast, adaptive challenges do not fall neatly into current structures. They fall across boundaries and require diverse perspectives. They demand questioning of each group's assumptions; experimenting with novel strategies; and adjusting people's values, habits, and priorities in order to make progress on the challenge.

When I worked for the government in Madagascar, governmental leaders clearly faced the adaptive challenge of halting the country's exponential population growth. The population had doubled over the previous twenty-five years, generating an enormous strain on the environment and resources of local communities. When a young couple married, they were given the blessing by their elders "May you have seven sons and seven daughters." This kind of practice, however, was not sustainable, and it posed an adaptive challenge for people to modify the value for large families. The practice had become maladaptive in the context of a changed world and threatened the sustainability of the already fragile economy and ecosystem.

But even outwardly simple, technical problems can have an adaptive component. When working in Madagascar, I saw a development project fail because of the lack of understanding for adaptive work. In this situation, NGO personnel had built a well and provided a water pump to the village because they thought it would solve a routine technical problem. The women in the village would spend considerable time daily fetching water from a distant river, and the intention of the well was to "fix the problem." The NGO believed the villagers would appreciate the well. However, some did not. After two weeks, the well and the water pump were destroyed. It was later discovered that it was the village women—the intended beneficiaries of the project—who had destroyed the well. Why? Because the well was an unwelcome disruption to their traditional pattern of living that included walking with their sisters and daughters in a daily ritual to fetch water. The new arrangement also meant that they had to spend more time in the village around their annoying men. No one had asked whether they wanted the well. Also, even if someone had asked, they might not have fully understood at that time how the change would impact the villagers' lives. Such is the nature of adaptive challenges: they have layers of complexity and often generate unpredictable surprises.

To mobilize people to address interdependent challenges and to do the adaptive work of change, you must work at the boundaries. You must be aware of visible and invisible boundaries that impede change and thwart shared progress. You must be able to cross boundaries to engage diverse groups in the work of problem solving and change. Sometimes, you must intervene to bust internal boundaries within your own group to open up the flow of information and get people to engage the outside world. For some problems, the leadership challenge is to help groups transcend their boundaries—to leave the safety of the known and to venture into the great unknown in pursuit of creativity and innovation. And there will be times when the leadership work is to help multiple groups bridge boundaries over deep divides in order to resolve conflicts, heal wounds, and reduce the mystery of the other in order to generate a mutually beneficial future.

To exercise leadership as a global change agent, you need to think about power differently. Even if you have considerable formal power, it will probably be insufficient to produce the change that you seek. Fernando Henrique Cardoso, the former president of Brazil, expressed the limitations of his power this way:

> I was always surprised at how powerful people thought I was. Even well-informed, politically sophisticated individuals would come to my office and ask me to do things that showed they assumed I had far more power than I really did. I always thought to myself, if only they knew how limited the power of any president is nowadays.[17]

You do not need formal, positional power to exercise leadership. Anyone can be a change agent, although in varying degrees and in varying ways, whether from the center or from the sidelines. Of course, some people have considerable power and can get attention easily and do big things. Some people have little power but can use what power they have to stand and be counted. They can raise an issue, challenge an assumption, and reach out to someone who is different, marginalized, or being harmed. They can support others in their leadership work. Even small interventions can sow seeds that may trigger dynamic change processes if the problem is ripe and the window of opportunity is seen and exploited. Consider Rosa Parks, whose refusal to move to the back of a bus in Montgomery, Alabama, in 1955 was a catalyzing action for the civil rights movement.[18] Her example underscores that what is critical is not how much power you have but the courageous, strategic, and creative use of your power.

Courage is needed to tap the internal strength to cross a boundary, raise an issue, and challenge a group. It is the willingness to make an intervention, to stand and be counted, and to engage in the work of change, particularly when others are hesitating, resisting, or fleeing. Strategy is needed to have a sense of when to intervene and where to intervene. It is needed to figure out when to provoke and when to evoke; to know when to move forward and when to be still; and to figure out who to partner with and who to avoid. And, creativity is needed to get attention. People are overwhelmed with so many activities and obligations. The change agent must intervene into a sea of competing concerns and often conflicting priorities to generate engagement and trigger a positive reaction and interest.

Are there people today providing effective leadership for a fractured world? Absolutely. Many people—with and without formal positional authority—are helping groups, companies, and communities address deep fissures, transcend differences, and tackle their toughest challenges.

Consider the fearless leadership of Malala Yousafzai, the teenager who was shot by the Taliban for promoting girls' right to go to school in the tribal areas of Pakistan. Today she is a powerful advocate for the education of girls all over the world.

In Barranquilla, Colombia, Manuel María Márquez, an ordinary citizen, is crossing boundaries to mobilize the civil society and the business community to work together to reduce government corruption; to build an educated, responsible citizenry; and to create a globally competitive city that provides equal opportunity for all and not just for the elites.

Some outstanding CEOs also personify this new form of leadership—men and women who are reinventing what it means to be in business and ensuring their companies are global in mindset and practice and can still create "delightful experiences" for the consumer in whatever part of the world they might be. Jeff Bezos at Amazon and Hiroshi Mikitani at Rakuten in Japan are examples of such change agent CEOs.

As a UN diplomat, Sérgio Vieira de Mello was the embodiment of the global change agent in his work rebuilding Lebanon, Cambodia, Kosovo, East Timor, and assisting a broken Iraq until his untimely death at the hands of terrorists in 2003. In terms of wielding faith and spirituality to help people cross deep divides, Pope Francis and the Dalai Lama are nothing short of remarkable.

Some of the most dynamic leadership, however, can be seen by mayors in cities and towns throughout the world who must be local change agents to create more cosmopolitan and globally oriented cities. One example is Joko Widodo, the former mayor of Surakarta, Indonesia. Rather than try to force change, as many other mayors had done, Widodo worked tirelessly with diverse groups to resolve practical problems the city faced. For one challenge, the city had a plan to relocate thousands of street vendors—some of the city's poorest residents—to designated locations. Widodo had more than 150 meetings with community members, city officials, bankers, and the street vendors themselves over four years, to learn about the complexity of the challenge, discover the aspirations of the varied groups, and to co-generate a workable solution. By virtue of Widodo's leadership in transitioning the initially resistant vendors successfully into the urban economic system, they now have government-provided carts and kiosks, free business licenses, sanitation training and support, and easy access to banks and lending cooperatives for finance to grow their businesses. The solution also resulted in a cleaner city, a reduction in traffic congestion and sanitation problems, and satisfied street vendors who now enjoyed better facilities and greater profits.[19] In 2014, Widodo, the former furniture businessman and mayor, was elected president of Indonesia. The hope is that he can do for his country what he did for his city.

In the following chapters, I will present the principles for exercising leadership and being a global change agent—principles derived from my interviews with or observations of the change agents just mentioned, and many more. Before you can fully engage in boundary work, however, you must diagnose the nature of the adaptive challenge and determine where groups are stuck—the topic of the next chapter.

LEADERSHIP FOR A FRACTURED WORLD
QUESTIONS FOR PRACTICE

1. What is the nature of the interdependent problems that your group faces?

2. What are the boundaries and fractures that separate groups that make shared problem solving difficult?

3. Do you see the manifestation of the tribal impulse? How does it get acted out? How might you contain it?

4. What are the notions of progress for yourself, your group, and other groups connected to the problems and challenges you face? Are there competing notions of progress?

5. How might the cultural drift—the taken-for-granted values, practices, and assumptions—serve to put people on autopilot, generate blind spots and biases, and reduce interdependent problem-solving capacity?

6. How might you be a global change agent and provide leadership to promote adaptive change and help groups address interdependent challenges?

CHAPTER 2

Diagnostic
Boundary Spanning

*Discovering Where and How
Groups Get Stuck*

To exercise leadership as a global change agent, you must
engage in diagnostic boundary spanning—analyzing and
crossing boundaries to discover features of the complexity
of the challenge and to learn where and how groups get stuck.
Too often people, thinking they are leading, launch a full-frontal
assault without appreciating the human and cultural dimension
of the problem and doing sufficient diagnostic work. They focus
on solutions prematurely, getting a partial diagnosis at best and
generating partial solutions with unintended consequences. If you
fail to do initial and ongoing diagnostic work of the group dynamics
and the environment, you might falter in your leadership efforts.

When I use the term *group*, I am using the term quite liberally
to mean a specific group, such as a work group; a large group, such
as a community or institution; or a social system comprised of
multiple factions that coalesce around a shared challenge.

The diagnostic process is like unpeeling layers of the onion, going from a superficial understanding to deeper insight about the group, its boundaries, the essence of the problem, and the perspectives of the different groups connected to the problem, with the objective to learn

- where the fractures, fissures, and fault lines exist, and why;
- where and how group boundaries and cultural practices impede problem solving and change; and
- what aspects of the group culture can be leveraged for change and used to promote adaptive problem solving, and what aspects need to be modified or discarded.

Diagnostic boundary spanning includes reconnaissance of the external environment and mapping of the terrain. Using the analogy of a camera, it is the process of "zooming out" with a wide-angle lens to see from a broader perspective. It is analyzing what is happening beyond group boundaries or at the frontier, and noticing emerging threats and opportunities such as new trends, changed conditions, and potential resource streams.

Diagnostic boundary spanning also requires "zooming in" to discover the reality on the ground. This aspect of the analysis is conducted close-up among the people to explore how they interpret the problem, why it persists, what their aspirations are, and what sacred values they cherish. It is an analysis of people's relationship to their group boundaries in the context of the interdependent problem or adaptive challenge.

To provide change agent leadership, you must be skilled at both zooming out to see the big picture and zooming in to see the specific details.[1] This is not a one-off activity but an ongoing process of discovery—learning more about the complexity of the challenge through direct engagement.

The first task of boundary spanning is to discover what is at stake for the group and why change is needed.

Determine What Is at Stake

A compelling case for change must be developed from the diagnosis of where and how groups are stuck. In creating that case, as a change agent, you must personally appreciate—and help others to appreciate—what is at stake if people do not change, if the problem persists, if the fracture expands, or if groups do not respond to an emerging threat or take advantage of a unique opportunity? What will be the loss? If nothing significant is to be gained or lost, then nothing really is at stake that would warrant the need for change or interdependent problem solving. However, if what is at stake is the very survival of the group, valuable parts of the group, or the bonds that hold diverse groups together, then the stakes are high, and a clear adaptive challenge lies before you.

In analyzing what is at stake, it is important to zoom out and look at the problem in the context of the larger system, and to zoom in to see potential dangers and losses for the people in the group. When the systemic and local realities are combined, the "what's at stake" question takes on greater significance.

For example, the stakes were very high when the Atlantic cod fishing industry collapsed in Newfoundland, Canada, in 1992. This industry had existed for more than three hundred years and powerfully shaped the lives of people on Canada's eastern coast. The government declared a moratorium on the fishing of cod because their numbers had been overfished, falling to 1 percent of their earlier level. The moratorium led to the largest industrial closure in Canada's history, with forty thousand workers becoming unemployed.[2]

Big man leadership, mismanagement, and modern technologies contributed to the collapse of the industry. Since so much money was to be made and so many communities were dependent on cod fishing for their livelihood, the government had neglected regulation of the industry, and foreign trawlers were allowed into the area. Advanced technology that produced larger and faster boats, longer and deeper nets, and the use of sonar to detect abundant schools of fish had made cod fishing extremely easy and profitable. In previous generations, it was estimated that approximately eight million tons of cod were caught over a hundred-year period. In the present day, the same number of cod can be caught in ten to fifteen years.[3]

Unsurprisingly, when the fishing communities were told that change was needed and their livelihood was at stake, they angrily reacted and went to the streets in protest. One furious mob actually confronted the minister for fisheries and demanded to know why there were no fish left in their waters and what he was going to do about it. The minister responded, "There's no need to abuse me, I didn't take the fish from the goddamn water."[4]

To this day, decades after the beginning of the moratorium, there is no sign of recovery. This issue has been a social, environmental, and economic tragedy.

To help a group avoid a major breakdown or disaster, the leadership challenge is to get people to face the reality of the consequences of their maladaptive practices on themselves and others, and on the larger system, before it is too late. Groups often do not think beyond the immediate confines of their parochial boundaries and immediate interests, and therefore they must be educated about how their practices generate negative consequences. Politics can also get in the way—as with the Newfoundland government that neglected engaging the fishermen, communities, and local authorities in anticipating dangers and working together to change their respective maladaptive practices.

Clarifying what is at stake is a critical part of diagnosing how the group can shift from being stuck in maladaptive practices and ill-suited narratives, to engaging in change as a means for addressing messy problems and generating progress.

Zoom Out: Recognizing Global Forces and Systemic Dynamics in the Background

Zooming out is what social scientists call "global processing."[5] It is like looking out into the horizon for oncoming storms or changed conditions. It is looking beyond your immediate world or group boundaries to see what is happening in the background that is generating the observable tensions and problems in the foreground. It is about seeing the larger system and how powerful external forces, trends, currents, and systemic dynamics are impacting what is happening locally as it pertains to generating problems, tensions, and fault lines in a group and between groups.

To appreciate the power of external forces to affect our lives at the local level, consider the analogy of ocean currents. Most people do not appreciate how ocean currents affect us beyond a day at the beach, but currents help regulate the world's climate and have important effects on marine life below the ocean's surface and all human life above the surface. For example, there are two kinds of ocean currents: deep currents and surface currents. Deep currents move both horizontally and vertically across the ocean floor and are connected throughout the world, creating what is known as the "great ocean conveyor belt." It takes these currents about one thousand years to complete one circuit. Surface currents flow horizontally above the deep ocean currents. Local shoreline

currents—the ones impacting our beach experience—are surface
currents that are influenced by local geography, the moon, weather,
and tides.[6]

If you are a meteorologist, a marine biologist, an environmental scientist, or a sailor, these data are immensely important to
you. Distinguishing between surface currents and deep currents,
and monitoring the direction and intensity of the flow, can help
you make predictions, understand patterns, and spot aberrant
dynamics—and thus use that information to develop strategies
to deal with potential threats.

As a change agent, you must seek to understand the forces and
currents in the background that are pushing and carrying groups
in various directions. "Deep currents" are global issues such as
population and migration trends, the dynamics concerning food
and water, environmental sustainability, the integrated global
economy, unresolved generational conflicts between groups, and
enduring cultural values. "Surface currents" include new and changing technologies, local politics and the local economy, and the
preferences and fashions of the day. If these background currents
are not taken into consideration in the work of change, stress
points, fault lines, and fissures will persist, causing unexpected
disruptions and breakdowns within the group and between groups.

The fishermen of Newfoundland, they did not zoom out to
appreciate how the currents in the larger environment were generating dynamics that threatened their livelihood in the long
run. They did not appreciate that technological advances in the
industry, such as longer and wider drift nets, sonar for finding
fish, and bigger and faster boats, could lead to overfishing. They
also did not appreciate that the deregulation of the industry, the
global demand for cod, and an influx of competitors from other
countries would exacerbate the problem. Because they were caught

up in the immediacy of their work, the fisherman failed to see how these systemic changes were generating powerful currents that would literally lead to the collapse of their industry.

But not all currents can be seen, anticipated, or predicted; sometimes they come out of nowhere. Divisions, fractures, and breakdowns in and between groups may be the product of disruptions in specific parts of a complex system that generate stresses in other parts. This is known as the "butterfly effect." The mathematician and meteorologist Edward Lorenz coined the term to describe what he saw in highly accurate computer models of weather systems: minute changes in initial conditions, as small as the wing-beat of a butterfly, can make the difference between whether or not a destructive tornado strikes a town.[7] The butterfly effect is all around us. War, natural catastrophes, pandemics, and economic collapse, for example, are common manifestations of once-small turbulences that set off a chain of events that may take many years and billions of dollars to unwind. Once panic sets in, people find it difficult to resist the forces of what seems to be inevitable.

Consider the case of Strauss, a multinational food and beverage company headquartered in Tel Aviv. It had to address problems generated by "global currents" and the "butterfly effect." Strauss is a well-managed company that makes excellent products that people value. It was one of the first companies in Israel to become a global company. Everyone was proud of Strauss—until recently.

In 2011, fractures emerged between the company and its customers. The trouble began when a young unemployed man started attacking the company on Facebook for selling its chocolates at a higher price in Israel than in the United States. Other consumers felt similarly cheated and started a movement against the company. A large group of mothers then joined the movement, demanding that Strauss lower the cost of baby's milk. Management tried to explain the realities of inflation and the costs of production, distribution, and marketing in a multinational business, but this approach did not work. The movement led to a boycott of the company's products and threats to the lives of some senior managers. Although Strauss was privately owned, the public even demanded to know the salaries of management and the financial details of the company.

The anti-Strauss campaign was launched by a single person, but soon thousands of people joined the movement, including some politicians, with the media fanning the flames. It was a movement with no one in charge, and disparate groups exploited it to their own advantage. I interviewed the chairwoman, Ofra Strauss, who told me she had never seen anything like this movement. Indeed, for the management of Strauss, this was a watershed moment: business would never be the same. Global economic currents, social media currents, and the currents of more savvy and demanding consumers all combined to spur unprecedented, even unreasonable, demands for the company to become more transparent and responsive. Strauss management would require a totally new model of leadership to respond to these challenges, as the old model did not consider dispersed power and the intensity of emerging currents. They realized that the company could no longer be managed as a closed system or take the consumer for granted. It now had to be managed as an open, dynamic system that could cross boundaries to diagnose and respond to sudden disruptions and shifting expectations with speed and sensitivity.

Human beings are generally not particularly good at attending to systemic, interdependent, and unpredictable problems, whether they are a product of global forces or sudden disruptions. The cultures of our respective groups, the roles we play in these groups, and the siloed structures of institutions often cause us to view problems through the narrow and myopic lens of immediate self- or group interest. As a result, groups are inclined to perpetuate fractures and add to existing problems. In providing leadership as a global change agent, the challenge is to study emerging global currents and to appreciate the implications for change at the local level but also to be vigilant for sudden and unpredictable shifts caused by the butterfly effect that generate new dangers as well as unique opportunities.

Zoom In: Determine What Is Adaptive and Maladaptive in the Group Cultural Drift

The anthropologist Clifford Geertz said that "man is an animal suspended in webs of significance he has spun for himself. I take culture to be those webs."[8] As you conduct your diagnostic work, you must understand enough about the webs of significance of the groups connected to the adaptive challenge so that you can determine where people might be trapped, what values might be maladaptive, and what values can be leveraged for change.

Fractures exist in groups and between groups because there is something deficient or maladaptive in their problem-solving processes. The deficiencies could be in their shared values, habits, practices, or priorities. The challenge for any group is to increase its adaptive capacity—the capacity to respond to changing conditions, new threats, and complex problems. If a group cannot respond successfully to critical and urgent inter-dependent challenges, there probably is something maladaptive in the group's cultural drift.

As I explained in Chapter 1, the group cultural drift provides a set of taken-for-granted assumptions, processes, and procedures for guiding action, solving routine problems, and addressing predict-able challenges. It might work well in most contexts when dealing with routine challenges, but it might be ineffective when dealing with complex, interdependent challenges because solutions lie outside the prevailing cultural drift. Unless the group can modify its cultural drift to address a novel or complex problem and adapt to changed circumstances, fractures will persist, problems will go unresolved, and a serious breakdown in the system could occur.

Analyze Group Cultural Narratives

As a change agent, you may not have the time or skill of an anthropologist to do a comprehensive cultural assessment, but you need to understand what is important to the different factions and to gain insight into the values, habits, practices, and priorities of the people connected to the challenge. The diagnostic task is to determine what is maladaptive in the drift that needs to be modified or discarded, and what is adaptive that can be harnessed to promote change.

A way to access adaptive and maladaptive values is by analyzing *group cultural narratives*. Narratives are the stories people tell that reinforce their boundaries. They are group stories that explain what is acceptable and unacceptable behavior for a member of the group. The story shapes people's identity, thinking, and actions. It is reinforced through myths, rituals, ceremonies, and rewards and punishments. When confronted with choices or problems, the group cultural narrative helps people decide on a particular approach. It is a powerful determinant of the horizon of possibility and the group's concept of progress. It is the group's story of the purpose of life and why they do what they do. It defines how they should live and how they should die.

The group narrative has two key dimensions: an orientation to time and an orientation to human relationships.

The Time Dimension: Yesterday, Today, and Tomorrow

The time dimension is important to understand because it is the collective group narrative around

- how people see and use the past,
- their sense of what is important to pursue in the present, and
- their relationship to the future.

Does the group feel they can shape their future? To what degree are people mired in the past? What are people's priorities in terms of where they invest time, resources, and effort?

The time dimension of the group narrative has three subnarratives: the narratives of yesterday, today, and tomorrow.

The narrative of yesterday

The *narrative of yesterday* is the story of the past. It highlights the accomplishments, sacrifices, and intentions of the founders and early members of the group, whether that story begins one year ago, one hundred years ago, or a thousand years ago. Some groups have very long yesterdays. The story of yesterday presents the trials and tribulations of a group's journey through time. It might include the evils perpetrated on them by others and their triumphs over adversity. It is the story of greatness, heroism, folly, and loss. It is the myths, fables, and events chosen carefully to define a group and provide a legacy that can be carried as a source of pride and identity into the future.

The narrative of yesterday might also include a maladaptive element that keeps a group mired in the past, resistant to change, and that perpetuates fractures between groups. The people might cherish the past more than pursuing their desired future or crossing boundaries to address collective problems. They might pine for a bygone era, or they might simply desire to be respectful of their predecessors. Sometimes it is tradition that keeps the group from progressing; sometimes it is past conflicts and grievances. The group's preoccupation with celebrating the honor, battles, or martyrdom of past members might perpetuate an identity that is maladaptive in the context of an urgent change challenge where bridges must be crossed, relationships cultivated, and a new identity constructed.

For the Newfoundland cod fishermen, their narrative of yesterday had a long history of more than three hundred years. They were doing the same work their fathers, grandfathers, and great-grandfathers had done. And, given their history, they believed there would always be an overabundance of fish, and it was difficult for them to imagine the possibility of a different reality—such as the depletion of their most valuable resource and a livelihood without fishing.

The narrative of today

The *narrative of today* is the story of what is important to attend to in the present. It is the story about the purpose of living and the purpose of work. What activities must be pursued in the present? This is the story that justifies the expense of energy and resources in the here and now. It is the measure of the good life. It is how a people hold themselves accountable at the end of each day for a job well done.

The narrative of today can be maladaptive when the story leads people to focus on a set of activities that have little to do with addressing emerging threats, changed conditions, or external forces and currents. And, by virtue of focusing on the wrong set of activities in the present, they make themselves vulnerable. Such was the case with Wall Street banks and the global financial crisis of 2008. The financial institutions' narrative of today exemplified a preoccupation with making fast money in the short term without considering the implications for the longer term or for the wider economy should the strategy fail—which it did.

The narrative of today might clash with other groups' activities, priorities, and narratives, producing deep fractures. But the narrative might also capture powerful values that are adaptive and that can be harnessed for driving change. A group might value hard work, for example, delayed gratification, and future-oriented education—all orientations that can be promoted to facilitate change.

For the fishermen of Newfoundland, their narrative of today was that they would always wake up each morning and go fishing. An abundant catch was the indicator that they were working and living honorably. It allowed them to feed their families, educate their children, and enjoy a sense of community. They did not want to pause to entertain the threats on the horizon that indicated the dangers of overfishing.

The narrative of tomorrow

The *narrative of tomorrow* is the story of the future, whether that future literally is tomorrow or a hundred years out. It tells the story of the group's dreams and aspirations in the context of time. Do they think long-term or short-term? What is their notion of progress? What does their future hold? What is their horizon of possibility? Can they shape the future, or does fate determine their future? Given the realities that they must face, does the narrative of tomorrow include sufficient aspiration to propel people forward to deal with impediments to progress and turn their dreams into reality?

How a group values the future has ramifications for where and how they invest their time and resources. When the future is expected to be better than the present, the group will have the motivation to invest in the future through infrastructure, savings, and education. If the narrative of tomorrow is absent or weak— meaning that the group does not have sufficient vision or energy to prepare for future challenges—the group might be inclined to waste resources. People might also become excessively focused on honoring the past or enjoying the present at the expense of planning for or creating their future. Thus, when dangers come their way or the need for change is urgent, they falter in response because they have not developed the capabilities, resources, and mindsets needed to succeed.

The narrative of tomorrow might be maladaptive in that it generates a set of aspirations and priorities for the group that clash with the aspirations and priorities of other groups, leading to conflicts in the present or the potential for conflict in the future. The group might have a compelling narrative of tomorrow, but it is maladaptive in the sense that it is unrealistic, even delusional, making it nothing more than a pipedream or a futile longing. The narrative might be exclusive and not inclusive: the group might see a future for itself that does not include other key groups. The Nazis of World War II, for example, had a narrative of tomorrow that emphasized an Aryan thousand-year empire devoid of Jews and other minorities.

When a group is attached to a narrative of tomorrow that is not appropriate for current realities, they will be in danger of losing much of the value and resources they have amassed because they will be wasting time and energy in pursuing a fantasy that tries to build a future on unrealistic assessments of the challenges they face. Nazi Germany was a diagnostic failure, as was the Soviet empire in its understanding of human nature and national and international economic realities. Absent a means to reality-test a narrative of tomorrow, people risk harm to themselves and others.

For the fishermen of Newfoundland, their narrative of tomorrow was the myth of endless abundance. They took for granted that they would be doing tomorrow what they were doing today and yesterday, and could continue to operate with the same practices and priorities. Given the lack of diagnostic boundary spanning and their delusional belief that the status quo would persist, they were shocked when the reality hit them and disrupted their stable world.

The Relationship Dimension: Me, My People, and Them

The relationship dimension of the group cultural narrative is about human relationships—the narratives of me, my group, and them. It is about

- how one perceives one's personal role and how much freedom one has to intervene, diverge from the norm, and create;
- the value and importance of the group in defining acceptable and appropriate behavior; and
- how other groups are perceived and related to—are they friend or foe, or simply a mystery?

The narrative of me

The *narrative of me* is the personal story the individual tells about who they are, what they can and cannot do, and the nature and limits of their boundaries. The narrative of me provides a set of injunctions and guidelines to live and work by for the individual. It is the story of individual agency. The story emphasizes how much space an individual has to take action, conduct experiments, and try new things. Are they bound by their role, obligations, and allegiances that constrain them and determine what they can and cannot do? Is individual self-expression encouraged or discouraged? How deeply is the narrative of me subsumed in group membership?

As a change agent, appreciating the narrative of me is important because it allows you to have a sense of what an individual can do within the confines of the group to address the problem. You might be asking people to voice their opinion, take risks, cross boundaries, and reach out to opponents; but if their narrative of me does not encourage individual agency and initiative, then it will be difficult, even impossible, for a person to transcend the clutches of the group because they fear being disloyal or violating group boundaries. On the other hand, you might be able to harness particular values of the narrative of me to energize individual agency on behalf of problem solving and change. In other words, the story might have ample room for maneuverability, creativity, and contribution.

The narrative of my people

The *narrative of my people* is the story of "my group"—whether the team, a professional group, the company, the community, or the nation. It is the story that explains what it means to be a member of a particular group, and who people are for one another in the context of that group. It defines roles, loyalties, obligations, and group boundaries.

The narrative of my people defines who *is* us. Is it the immediate family, the extended family, or the tribe? At work, is it your immediate team or your department? In Chapter 1, I mentioned how an overseas office of a multinational software company was not being included in the problem-solving processes of the headquarters in the United States. The narrative of my people in the headquarters did not really include the overseas office.

People belong to many groups, and each group might have a distinct narrative and boundary. The narrative that is activated at any moment depends on the context and the challenge being faced.

The narrative might have maladaptive elements emphasizing excessively tight boundaries that do not facilitate the free flow of information, people, and resources. When such is the case, the group might become narrow-minded and oblivious to what is going on in the larger world. When the narrative of my people is excessively parochial, the group's bonds can be very tight, and a strong sense of community can result—but at a cost. The group may grow suspicious of the larger world or denigrate the outsider, which in turn can lead people to try to solve their problems alone, becoming reluctant to build bridges between groups and establish partnerships.

Another maladaptive aspect of the narrative of my people might be excessive narcissism, which is an inflated sense of self-importance or superiority. In other words, the group might feel unduly special and far better than everyone else. This fantasy might lead them to be lax in terms of monitoring their environment, pursuing change, upgrading their capacities, or learning from others.

The flip side of narcissism—also a maladaptive element—is the feeling of inferiority, insignificance, or marginalization. The group might feel that they are just another group like any other group and there is nothing special or unique about them, and thus they have no real contribution to make or anything of value to offer. If the group feels inferior, members of the group can easily flee from the change challenge because they feel little connection to or responsibility for the larger system. Group members might think, "Why bother?" and conclude that sacrificing or working hard to address the problem is not worth the effort. If they feel suppressed, oppressed, or marginalized, their frustrations might even lead them to act out in negative ways, as happened in Ferguson, Missouri, in August 2014, when race riots broke out over the controversial killing of an African American man by a white police officer.

The narrative of the other

The *narrative of the other* is the story of people outside the group— those people who are not us. This story gives guidance on how to treat the other and what that relationship should look like. In a company, the internal other could be other divisions or departments; the external other could be customers and competitors. In a religion, the other could be other faiths or nonbelievers.

The other could be the people who do not share your values or your narrative, and thereby are perceived as a threat to your group's well-being or interests. It could be the people across the river or the people across the ocean. It might be the people in the office across the hallway or the people on another floor. The other is the group that is different, that has a competing agenda or values that might, if you get too close, pollute your group or make life difficult.

Frequently, the narrative of the other is the story of blame. It is the story the group relates about how terrible the other group is and all the bad things they have done or might do. The narrative of the other is sometimes merged with the narrative of yesterday. Serbians, for example, remember the Battle of Kosovo that occurred in 1389. This battle, between the Orthodox Christian Serbs and the attacking Muslim Ottomans, is particularly important for Serbian national identity to this day. The Serbs were annihilated, and their lands became subsumed under the Ottoman Empire. The pain of humiliation and defeat was exploited six hundred years later by Serbian president Slobodan Milošević when he invoked the Battle of Kosovo in his famous speech on the anniversary of the battle on June 28, 1989. Calling for the assertion of Serbian nationalism, the speech inflamed other groups in the region, particularly Bosnians and Albanians, leading to a period of brutal warfare, ethnic cleansing, and the eventual breakup of Yugoslavia.[9]

The narrative of the other is maladaptive when the group scapegoats another group and refuses to examine its own responsibility for contributing to the problem. It is maladaptive when the group refuses to let go of the past, heal old wounds, and move on. The pain lingers, passing from one generation to the next, and the fractures become ever more powerful psychological divides that make collaborative problem solving and creative work difficult.

As a change agent, you must seek to understand how the narrative of the other emerged. What is it in the relationship between groups that has generated this divide? How do people explain the fracture? Does it have a long history, or is it a recent occurrence? What do people do to perpetuate the divide?

The narrative of the other might be weak or even absent when groups are a mystery to one another. Groups can be like ships passing each other in the night, recognizing they exist but never caring to connect at a deeper level. They might be so preoccupied with attending to their own interests and immediate concerns that they have little idea of what the other group is doing. When no one is talking to or interacting with the other group, the potential for mistrust, suspicion, and conflict is ever present, particularly when the need for problem solving has emerged because of an interdependent challenge.

The narrative of the other is not all bad, however. It can also have many adaptive features. For example, the story might describe complementary capacities, shared values, and common priorities that can be harnessed to generate connections, advance shared problem solving, and promote the work of change.

Determine What Boundary Work Is Needed to Make Progress on the Adaptive Challenge

Upon doing your analysis and piecing together group narratives, you will have a better sense of where people are stuck and the nature of the fractures and divisions that impede progress. You will have a better appreciation of how people define themselves, their group, and other groups in the context of the interdependent challenge. You will also have a sense of how people define their boundaries—where those boundaries are and their strength and permeability. And you will likely know more about what values and practices have become maladaptive and need to change, and what values and practices are adaptive and can be leveraged to promote interdependent problem solving and change.

The diagnostic work will also reveal (1) what boundaries need to be crossed and who needs to cross those boundaries to engage the challenge; and (2) whether the boundaries need to be expanded, busted, transcended, or have bridges built over deep fractures, in order to help people to do the requisite problem solving and creative work to produce systemically beneficial change.

Boundary work is difficult work because it necessitates reinterpreting boundaries and aspects of identity and belonging. It requires reframing the current narrative or co-creating a new narrative. It involves loss, but it also involves learning, growth, and gain. It necessitates moving people out of arenas of comfort into arenas of discomfort on behalf of adaptive work. The following chapters share specific principles for how to provide change agent leadership—with sensitivity, strategy, and skill—to address fractures and orchestrate interdependent problem solving and change.

DIAGNOSTIC BOUNDARY SPANNING QUESTIONS FOR PRACTICE

1. What is the adaptive challenge or interdependent problem that needs to be addressed? What is at stake if the challenge is not productively addressed and the fracture persists?

2. Zooming out: What are the global, systemic forces and currents in the background impacting the problem that you see in the foreground? What threats, fractures, tensions, and opportunities do these forces and currents generate?

3. Zooming in: What is the reality on the ground? Where are groups stuck? What realities are people avoiding?

4. What are the narratives of the different factions, and what do they reveal about the problem, fractures, boundaries, and possibilities for change?

5. What are the maladaptive values, practices, and perspectives of the groups connected to the challenge that thwart interdependent problem solving and change?

6. What are the adaptive values, practices, and perspectives that can be leveraged to promote problem solving and change?

PART 2

Leadership in Action

CHAPTER 3

Crossing Boundaries

Helping Different Groups Address Interdependent Problems

To provide leadership for a fractured world, you will need to cross boundaries to mobilize diverse groups to participate in the work of multidimensional problem solving and change—professional, structural, cultural, religious, geographic, economic, class, and ethnic boundaries, to name but a few. Specifically, crossing boundaries is needed when

- a group faces an interdependent problem that involves other groups;
- multiple factions must come together to generate a systemic change;
- an exciting opportunity is available if diverse groups can collaborate.

Boundary-crossing work is important for governments that must create collaborative partnerships with the private sector to address community challenges pertaining to education, job creation, health care, and environmental protection initiatives. It is important for educational leaders who must mobilize the community, teachers, administrators, and politicians to support systemic reforms. It is much-needed work for the authority figures of religious institutions, to convene diverse faiths to share lessons and perspectives to address some of our toughest problems, including alienation, terrorism, and warfare. And it is critical for senior executives of companies who must get people to transcend silos to create new products and services that best meet evolving consumer tastes.

In crossing boundaries, you must get groups, often with big differences and competing cultural narratives, to come together to appreciate the systemic nature of the problem, build a relational bridge, and adjust their values, practices, and priorities on behalf of adaptive change. You need to hold the disparate groups together long enough for shared problem solving to occur even though their natural instinct is to flee from the work or to blame the other.

One of the people I interviewed to talk about their toughest leadership challenges was Mary Robinson, the former United Nations high commissioner for human rights. In 2001 she organized an international conference on racism and xenophobia in Durban, South Africa. More than eighteen thousand people from around the globe came together to participate in a conversation on how to generate greater tolerance and acceptance in the world. She wanted each country to look within to see what they could do to advance toward a more inclusive society. The conference, however, was controversial. Certain groups, rather than look within, looked without. African nations wanted America and Europe to apologize for slavery. Arab nations declared Israel a racist state. Many groups used the conference to advance their own agenda;

and as a result, the U.S. delegation walked out of the conference after two days, and the European delegation also threatened to leave. Robinson did the best she could to hold the event together, and some very important work did get done—but it was difficult given the deep fractures that existed. Even a conference organized to reduce the fractures that divide us became for many groups a very fracturing event.

Crossing boundaries can be fraught with danger and volatility. No matter how powerful you are within the confines of your own group, the moment you cross a boundary into another group, your power and authority carry little weight, and people may ignore you. Therefore, in providing leadership you must be sensitive and strategic in order to navigate the political territory of competing interests and agendas of different groups.

To illustrate the demands and opportunities of crossing boundaries, consider the case of Michelle Rhee and her attempt to fix a broken school system and help it become world class.

Michelle Rhee's Attempt to Fix a Broken School District

Michelle Rhee was asked by Mayor Adrian Fenty to be the superintendent of schools for Washington, D.C. She took the job reluctantly because she knew it would be a difficult challenge. She had never been a superintendent before, although she had been a teacher and knew what was needed to make classrooms come alive with learning. She was also worried that she was an outsider—she was a Korean American with a Harvard master's degree, and the D.C. public school community was predominantly African American and poor. In addition, this challenge would be particularly daunting because the school district was one of the lowest performing in the nation as it pertained to test scores and attendance measures.[1] The school system, for all intents and purposes, was broken, but Rhee had a good sense on how to go about fixing it—so she believed.

Rhee knew that as an outsider, she needed the community's support, and she also knew that the church was central in the African American community, so that was where she went. At the Bible Way Church, Reverend Cornelius Showell invited Rhee to speak to his congregation to tell them who she was and to present her vision. Rhee stood at the pulpit, and this is what she said:

> The schools in our city have been failing our children for far too long. The only people who have paid the price for these failing schools have been the kids. I am committed to changing the way we educate our children. . . . It will require tremendous change. I'm going to need the entire community to help me. It can't happen only within the four walls of the school building. I need to work hand in hand with you. I ask for your prayers.

The congregation stood, cheered, and said "Amen!" They liked Rhee's spirit.[2]

Rhee was a visionary who did not hesitate in crossing racial, religious, socio-economic, or political boundaries. Her personal commitment was to fix an ailing school system so that every child had the best opportunity for a first-rate education, irrespective of their color or economic condition. She launched a comprehensive process of change; and, for her, it was a moral crusade. Her bold approach generated national attention. She appeared on the front page of *Time* magazine holding a broom, suggesting that she was sweeping the house clean.[3] She was also featured in the award-winning documentary *Waiting for Superman*, in which she was actually filmed firing a principal. She was a very public reformer, genuinely trying to get people to do the right thing and give greater attention to the quality and process of educating children.

Not everyone appreciated her, however. In her third year, even though student performance measures were starting to show significant improvement, Rhee was fired. The community had turned against her. The other casualty was her champion, Mayor Adrian Fenty. He lost his bid for reelection because of his support for Rhee and his advocacy for the reform agenda. Months after leaving the job, Rhee's husband asked her a rhetorical question: "Why, in a city with the worst public schools in the nation, would people turn against a mayor and a chancellor who were actually starting to improve their schools? Why reject them?"[4]

Due to her singular focus and crusader-like energy, Rhee made many enemies. She faced a complex adaptive challenge that required interdependent problem solving and the shifting of the values of multiple groups, yet she was inclined to approach it as a technical challenge by firing teachers and administrators she deemed incompetent. In her first year alone, she closed 23 community schools, fired 36 principals, and cut more than 120 central office jobs. In her second year, she fired 241 teachers and put 737 employees on notice.[5]

While her aims were noble, her tough, take-no-prisoners style generated significant opposition. She was viewed as an outsider and a threat to the status quo, and many people became defensive—defensive about being made wrong, defensive about their jobs, defensive about their community, and defensive about being forced to change—so they fought back.

Crossing boundaries to mobilize diverse factions to face an interdependent adaptive challenge is demanding and risky work. You have to work with diverse groups with competing agendas to generate a shared understanding of the challenge and to promote ownership of the problem. In doing so, you will be vulnerable. Any group at any time might seek to neutralize your leadership, thereby neutralizing the problem-solving process. Your challenge, therefore, rather than crusading, threatening, or forcing change, is to orchestrate, among the different factions, a process of learning, experimentation, and discovery. That process necessitates navigating messy political dynamics, competing group cultural narratives, and overt and covert opponents. What follows in this chapter is advice for increasing your chances for success.

Manage Your "Ugliness"

You must realize that in crossing boundaries to orchestrate change, not everyone will welcome you with open arms. Some might greet you with guns—figuratively or literally. Therefore, you must seriously consider what threat or blessing you represent to the different factions connected to the problem. Your challenge is to ensure that you are not perceived as being "ugly"—not too ugly, at least.

In 1958, a former American foreign service officer, William Lederer, wrote a fascinating novel with his colleague Eugene Burdick called *The Ugly American*. It was later turned into a film starring Marlon Brando. The story is about an imaginary Southeast Asian country that has a growing nationalist movement seeking to rid the country of foreign interference and gain political independence. The Americans, however, try to manipulate the nation's politics to their advantage but wind up making many mistakes and adding fuel to the fire—thus the title, *The Ugly American*.

Any person in any group and from any country can be guilty of being ugly. From a cultural point of view, the ugly individual is blatantly ethnocentric, and imperialistic in style and approach. Ethnocentrism is cultural self-centeredness, the belief that one's group is superior to another group.[6] Ethnocentric individuals interpret and evaluate other groups' behavior based on the application of their own standards and preferences. They make little effort to modify their behavior to suit the cultural environment in which they are operating, because they see no need to do so. Those with imperialistic tendencies are inclined to expand their territory or to impose their agenda, values, or perspectives on others to advance their own group's interests, without consideration for the contextual realities.

We all have ethnocentric tendencies, and perhaps a dash of an imperialistic nature. As a change agent, you must realize that your own cultural narrative and group loyalties at times might cause you to engage in tribalizing behavior, distort your perspective, and reduce your ability to listen and connect with another group's cultural narrative and interests, thereby leading some to accuse you of being ugly.

For anyone who crosses boundaries to exercise leadership, it might be impossible to escape fully from the evaluation of being ugly, particularly by discontented groups who regard you as a threat and thereby seek to thwart change. Therefore, it is important, to the degree possible, to manage the perception of ugliness and determine how ugly you are willing to be.

Sometimes playing the role of the ugly outsider is helpful, particularly when group members find it difficult to play that role because they fear being perceived as a troublemaker or as being disloyal. Management consultants, for example, can say things that others cannot say because they do not have a direct stake in the outcome or are not involved in organizational politics. More typically, however, it is important that you not be the one that names other groups' behavior as maladaptive or wrong. The behavior might well be negative, but people must come to that conclusion on their own, with your prompting by putting the consequences of their behavior before them. If you name their behavior as negative, you might be ignored or dismissed as being insensitive or ugly, and you thereby might miss an opportunity to get the group to take ownership of the problem.

To reduce the danger of being perceived as ugly, disrespectful, or judgmental, you need to cross boundaries with sensitivity and care. You need to have a sense of how your own cultural narrative and group biases inform your interpretation of the problem and your intervention strategies. And you need to cross boundaries quietly rather than with guns blazing.

The way the Americans intervened in Japan after World War II is an example of effective cross-boundary leadership. Leading the process, General Douglas MacArthur ensured that he and his fellow Americans were not perceived as a threatening occupying force, but as partners with the Japanese to transition the country back to a stable, functioning, and independent state. He succeeded.[7] For the most part, the cultural narrative of the Japanese people was honored. MacArthur knew that there were valuable aspects in that narrative pertaining to learning, harmony, discipline, and hard work that could be harnessed to support the work of change. He saw his role as primarily managing the boundaries so that the Japanese could do their own work of rebuilding the country. Even though there were factions in the United States that demanded the removal of the emperor, MacArthur personally met with him eleven times, acknowledging his sacred and symbolic role as a unifying figure for all Japanese. In 1951, MacArthur told Congress, "The Japanese people . . . have undergone the greatest reformation recorded in modern history. With a commendable will, eagerness to learn, and marked capacity to understand, they have from the ashes left in war's wake . . . created a truly representative government committed to the advance of political morality, freedom of economic enterprise, and social justice."[8] Had it not been for MacArthur's wise cross-boundary leadership, the situation could have been explosive.

In taking responsibility for how you are perceived and ensuring that you do not play the role of savior, hero, crusader, or conqueror, you must know what values to champion and what values to challenge. As a change agent, you walk a fine line between being respectful and disrespectful. You should not be overly respectful of all aspects of the culture and values of the groups you interact with, but at the same time not be disrespectful. If you are disrespectful, you will be rejected. But if you are excessively deferential in order to ingratiate yourself to another group and to be liked by them, then it might be difficult to challenge them to change or to make the sacrifices needed to address a shared adaptive problem.

Crossing Boundaries to Address Child Malnutrition in the American South

To illustrate the challenge of being responsible for what blessing or curse you represent when crossing boundaries, consider the case of a young Dr. Robert Coles and his experience working on poverty issues in America's Deep South in the 1960s.

Dr. Coles, of Harvard University, and his colleague Dr. Milton Senn, an experienced pediatrician and Yale professor, completed a major study on child malnutrition. Their findings were disturbing: in parts of the South, particularly Mississippi, children were suffering from levels of malnutrition and illnesses generally associated with people in Third World countries. They wrote a detailed report and sent their findings to key members of Congress and senior officials in the government, but few people showed any interest—except for Senator Robert Kennedy.

Kennedy told the doctors that he agreed with their conclusions and asked them what they intended to do about it. They said, "We've done all we can do." After a long pause, Kennedy countered, "I'm not so sure." He tried to help the doctors understand that if they were serious about change, they had to do more than simply send a report to political officials and government bureaucrats—the report would be too easy to ignore. Kennedy worked with them to develop and implement a strategy for getting sustained attention on the problem and to vicariously influence the group cultural narrative for progressive change.

"You folks are going after people with this report of yours," Kennedy said, "people who want to defend the status quo, even medical people in those places you visited—you shouldn't forget that."[9] He told them that they needed to appreciate the reality that they would be perceived as outsiders from elite universities in the Northeast, and many Southerners, especially white politicians and the medical establishment, would not take kindly to the two doctors' pejorative assessment of their community. Kennedy asked them to imagine how the people in Boston would feel if doctors from Mississippi strolled through their neighborhoods and then wrote a scathing public report that was an indictment on the health system, parents, politicians, and government officials responsible for public health.

To ensure that their interventions were even more potent with a Southern audience, Kennedy suggested ways to work with Southern politicians. He recommended that another member of their team, Dr. Raymond Wheeler, be the public face when speaking to the Senate and the media, because he was from the South. Wheeler was not an Ivy League type like Coles and Senn, and he could answer questions and address concerns with colloquial language and mannerisms that Southern people could more easily relate to.[10]

Kennedy helped the doctors understand what was required in taking a technical report on child malnutrition and turning it into a powerful intervention that could move people to face the reality of the problem and begin the work of change. He helped them navigate the complex political and cultural terrain of the U.S. Congress and the factional interests in the South. And he helped them manage their ugliness by not coming across as arrogant and judgmental. Coles later wrote about what the partnership with Kennedy was like:

> He made me anxious and showed me the pragmatic, politically astute side of him that in my gross naiveté I had not been prepared to see. He was bringing us down from our highfalutin innocence and idealistic moral high ground. He had from the start spotted a certain smugness in us, a conviction on our part that we knew exactly what we were talking about and that accordingly we ought to be heeded. . . . Hence, the polite assault on our self-pity, our failure to look realistically at why we'd been fended off, our inclination to take the whole matter personally, whether by impugning the motives of others or threatening to pull back our initial lobbying effort amidst declarations of inadequacy.[11]

To reduce the danger of groups using their evaluation of your ugliness as a reason not to face the problem, remember that you are rarely seen as a neutral arbiter of change. You must carefully consider how you will be perceived and, to the degree that it is possible, manage that perception.

Find Partners to Navigate the Terrain

In crossing boundaries, you are entering into terrain of *the other*. You need a network of partners to help you navigate the terrain, provide critical feedback, make interventions, and sustain the work of change. It is impossible to understand the complexities of an interdependent challenge through the lens of your own group narrative. You must seek diverse and even competing perspectives to generate a richer understanding of the system. Partners help you think through your options, broaden your perspective, and help you see what you cannot see from where you stand or from the limitations of your particular group narrative. Therefore, your network of partners should come from each of the factions in the system. Partners become fellow change agents and supporters. They can be the voice of encouragement and the voice of warning. They can help you carry the burden of responsibility.

Michelle Rhee, as an educational reformer, would have benefited by having partners to help her think through her options and the consequences of her choices. She made too many controversial decisions. For example, she fired a well-liked principal of one of the better schools in the city, a decision that stunned the community. Rhee failed to explain the justification of her action. This move only served to heighten class and ethnic tensions in the community, with one leading community member suggesting that the principal "was toppled" because a small group of "dissatisfied and largely affluent Anglo parents" were able to convince Rhee that she should go. A journalist noted that

> Rhee seemed to have no sense that in the District's Black community there is a great deal of sensitivity in being dictated to by those who think they know better. Until the late 1970s the City was ruled by a combination of congressional committees, often in the hands of blatant racists, and by non-elected appointed commissioners who showed little regard for those they ruled. . . . In this city, everything revolves around race,

class, and neighborhoods, and it makes no small difference that Rhee is an upper-middle-class Korean American from suburban Ohio, overseeing a system that is more than 80 percent black and overwhelmingly poor.[12]

Rhee was a talented and extraordinary educator who had devoted her life to helping inner-city children. She believed that every child, regardless of race or economic status, had the right to a first-rate education. In many ways, Rhee was a gift to the community. However, she was inclined to treat the work of change as a technical problem, applying her dictates, solutions, and expertise, rather than as an adaptive challenge, seeking a much deeper—and necessary—level of community engagement and partnership. Rhee's expertise was in teaching in the classroom, not in mobilizing diverse groups to deal with the politics of change. She was in over her head and needed people to help her think through her choices and the implications for the community.

Someone Rhee might have partnered with was Marion Barry, the seventy-year-old former four-time mayor of Washington, D.C. Barry, an African American, was elected as president of the school board in the 1970s, and served as mayor from 1979 to 1991, and then again from 1995 to 1999. Active in the civil rights movement in the 1960s, he was the first prominent civil rights activist to become the mayor of a major city in the United States. To many of people in D.C., he was a hero, even though he had spent time in jail for drug-related offenses. During Rhee's tenure, Barry was a member of the city council and a representative of Ward 8, a poor African American section of the city. He was not the power broker that he used to be, but he remained a force to be reckoned with.

When Rhee took the job, Barry invited her to drive with him around the city. "You don't know Ward 8, but you have to know

Ward 8," he told her. "Come with me." Rhee was reluctant to get in the car with Barry and told him that she would follow in her own car. "Nonsense, get in," he insisted. And with that invitation, or command, Rhee embarked on a tour of Ward 8. He drove her from school to school, pointing out different landmarks along the way. "You can't just close schools. That's not the way things work here," he said. "You need to understand the community. These schools are anchors of the community, like me. I know the community; I am the community; that's why they love me."[13]

Rhee was dismissive of Barry. She hesitated to partner with him because she saw him as being a part of the problem. To her, he perhaps embodied the old political establishment of the city who did little to address real community problems. A year later, when Barry and other city council members heard via the local newspaper, rather than from Rhee herself, that schools in his district were closing, he sent the message to Rhee that this decision was "unfair, wrong, and disrespectful." He added, "I urge you to fully involve the Council and the community in a true partnership so that we can all keep our focus on the children."[14]

Rhee did not partner with the city council. She saw politics as time-consuming, exasperating, and a distraction from her reform work. She later said, "If collaboration is the most important thing in your end goal, the only way to make a whole lot of people happy is to not change anything. But if you want to change things, the fact is there will be a group of people mad at you."[15] Rhee is right: if you are going to change anything, there will be unhappy people. However, time must be invested in cultivating cross-boundary partnerships to expedite and deepen the work of change. Partners help champion the work, protect the work, protect your resources, and protect you. They are essential, particularly in fighting the battles of systemic change.

Partners can also help you think through strategies for fighting battles as well as the consequences of those battles, and ensure you do not squander time and resources fighting unnecessary and wasteful battles. Robert McNamara said that he and President Kennedy had failed to use French president Charles de Gaulle as a partner in thinking through whether the Vietnam War needed to be fought. Vietnam was a former French colony, and Ho Chi Minh's forces undertook a lengthy, costly war to oust the French. The French knew the mindset and aspirations of the Vietnamese better than anyone, certainly better than the Americans. De Gaulle offered to broker a neutral government in Saigon. Of this offer, McNamara wrote:

> The deal de Gaulle had in mind would . . . have been in everyone's interest, including ours, for it would have allowed us to exit that conflict before it became an American war with tragic results that are well-known. But we refused even to consider de Gaulle's participation. We distrusted his motives. Some disliked him personally. But mostly, we thought—wrongly, as I now believe—we knew better than he did.[16]

A network of partners increases the chance that wiser heads prevail and reduce the risk of bad decisions due to bias, misinformation, misinterpretation, or miscalculation. It increases the possibility that good choices are made and strategies are pursued based on more informed choice, a sensible strategy, and a logical moral foundation.

Partnering in Iraq

In navigating the problem-solving terrain of a complex adaptive challenge, partners help you distinguish the factions embedded in the system. When operating alone, it is impossible to see and understand the disparate groups, competing values, different interests, and political dynamics of the wider social system.

Paul Bremer, in 2003, was sent to Iraq by the U.S. government to be their representative and to assist in the transition to democracy. Bremer had never done this kind of leadership work before—in fact, few people had. He was in unfamiliar terrain, his blind spots were abundant, and the burden was overwhelming. There was, however, one person in Iraq who was perhaps one of the most experienced professionals in the world pertaining to transitioning conflict-ridden nations: the United Nations representative, Sérgio Vieira de Mello.[17]

Vieira de Mello's most recent assignment had been heading the UN transitional process in East Timor, and from all accounts he did an extraordinary job. He had also led UN operations in Kosovo and Cambodia. He had been in the thick of some of the worst conflicts of recent years. Bremer, however, did not fully appreciate what Vieira de Mello had to offer. Although the two men had occasional meetings, Bremer viewed the UN agenda with suspicion and tried to keep Vieira de Mello and his people at a distance.

According to Samantha Power in her biography of Vieira de Mello, "he knew that in the three key areas where the Coalition was floundering—power sharing, policing, and economic development—the UN had made grave mistakes but had amassed unique and valuable expertise. Yet, to his amazement, the Coalition seemed uninterested in tapping it."[18] Vieira de Mello personally went out into the field and met with heads of key religious and political factions who had their own narratives and perspectives around the problem. But Bremer did not make a concerted effort to make Vieira de Mello and the UN team his partners in bringing democracy to Iraq. Consequently, the two men competed with each other over the same turf of war-torn Iraq. If they could have formed a working partnership, they might have helped each other see what neither could see as separate individuals in separate teams. As it was, Vieira de Mello and his team did their best to coordinate with the native Iraqi factions, while Bremer and his team tried to bring democracy to Iraq by imposition, dismantling the Iraqi army and outlawing the formerly dominant Ba'ath Party in all of its forms. Sadly, Vieira de Mello was killed when the UN headquarters was bombed in August 2003. Bremer left Iraq nine months later, and Iraq descended into bloody chaos.[19]

Make It Their Work, Not Yours

The purpose of providing cross-boundary leadership is not to do the work for people but to get others to be responsible for doing the demanding adaptive work themselves. As a change agent, you must orient people toward the work. People have to appreciate what is at stake if the situation of irresolution is not brought to resolution. You must engage each faction that owns a piece of the problem, working with them to make the necessary adjustments in their respective group narratives, perspectives, and priorities. Each faction can provide insight into the nuances and specifics of the problem, and their ideas can be instrumental in adding velocity to the work of change and ownership for the challenge.

No matter how passionate you are, unless the different factions can embrace or create a shared narrative or aspiration that is inclusive and realistic, change will be elusive, and some groups might try to subvert your leadership. Therefore, even though some factions might be perceived as opponents, you will need to think very carefully about the consequences of excluding them from participating in the work of change. If a group is excluded, people might feel they have to unjustly bear a heavy loss. All groups must invariably suffer some loss in adaptive change, and leadership is needed in helping people sustain their losses and transition to a new reality.

Paul Bremer, as head of the Coalition Authority in Iraq, might have made greater progress if he had understood this principle. One of Bremer's first decisions, informed by his consultation with Secretary of Defense Donald Rumsfeld and his faction, was to fire three hundred thousand Iraqi civil servants and military personnel who were associated with the regime of Saddam Hussein and the Ba'ath Party.[20] This order was in contrast to the pre-invasion plan to only dismiss those officers and officials most loyal to Saddam since Iraqis who wished to be teachers, police officers, or civil servants were required to belong to the Ba'athist party. Colin Powell, the U.S. secretary of state at the time, believed Bremer made a grave mistake:

> We were planning to eliminate top party leaders from posi-
> tions of authority. But lower-level officials and workers had the
> education, skills, and training needed to run the country. . . .
> Instead, Rumsfeld and Bremer disbanded the Army and fired
> Baath Party members down to teachers. We eliminated the very
> officials and institutions we should have been building on, and
> left thousands of the most highly skilled people in the country
> jobless and angry—prime recruits for insurgency.[21]

Bremer's decision, combined with the actions of a small group of carefully selected politicians and officials who were predom-inantly Shia, served to marginalize the Sunni faction and frac-ture the country further. Had Bremer and his team developed an appreciation of the deeper historical currents, factional divides, group cultural narratives, and the social and institutional structures that could maintain some continuity and facilitate the transition, they might have realized that they would be stirring up a hornet's nest by eliminating a major faction that needed to be included in the work of change.

Of course, no matter how hard you try, some factions might never support the work of change; they might even go to battle to thwart progress. Indeed, in taking on a complex adaptive challenge that involves many factions, you should anticipate opposition, resistance, and even occasional battles. But even when the opposition is significant and a battle must be pursued, you must be careful not to make it *your* battle—it must be *the group's* battle. If it is your battle, you will be perceived as a crusader, someone who is hell-bent on getting what you want at any cost. Of course, the people will need your help. The leadership task is to orchestrate the battle in such a way that it allows people to grapple with the problem, their competing notions of progress, and the implications of their values, practices, and priorities for the community as it pertains to addressing the adaptive challenge and generating change.

Michelle Rhee made the battle for educational reform *her* battle. In response, the opposition brought out their big gun, Randi Weingarten, the president of the largest teachers' union in the United States, to personally lead the fight against Rhee and her reforms. The union wanted no part of her program that encouraged a meritocratic reward system for teachers as they saw it ideologically in opposition to their need to protect the jobs of teachers. In fact, a member of Weingarten's camp explained to me that they had pictures of Rhee in their office, describing her as public enemy number one. It became an ugly battle, with the

union, through advertisements and campaigns, doing what it could
to discredit Rhee personally.[22] While battles can generate national
attention—in Rhee's case, by promoting debate on the state of
American schools—they can also easily become distractive and
destructive, displacing the adaptive work of change and leading
to great casualties.

To ensure that counterproductive battles are not fought, you
must acknowledge the difficulty for many group members to
accommodate a new position and give up deeply held beliefs and
truths about how the world should work and what their roles
should be. Indeed, you must realize that initially few people will
support you in the great leap forward, in spite of the logic of your
argument and the passion with which you present it. Therefore,
the work must be done in stages and through experimentation.
You must acknowledge the losses that some factions might
need to sustain, providing sufficient leadership to help them
sustain the loss, make adjustments, and orchestrate a successful
transition.

Manage the Boundary Keepers

Every faction has boundary keepers—powerful people whose role
is to protect their group's interests and defend the prevailing group
narrative. They are generally big man leaders—formal and informal
authority figures—who see it as their responsibility to protect
group boundaries, fight group battles, and minimize disruption
to the status quo, even if it means neutralizing the change agent.
Even chimpanzees have boundary keepers—powerful males that
patrol the boundaries and are known to kill intruding chimps
from other groups.[23]

As a change agent, you need to appreciate the role of boundary keepers and do your best to enroll them. They carry a heavy burden in being responsible for protecting the interests of their faction and maintaining boundaries. Their loyalties and obligations are to their group, and it is difficult for them to go back to their people and announce that change is needed and sacrifices must be made. Should they do so, they might be seen as disappointing their own people and failing to protect them from undue stress, and thus risk losing their authority.

While some boundary keepers will regard you as a threat to the prevailing order, others might listen and help you see the complexity of the challenge and identify subfactions that could be supporters of change. Some boundary keepers might agree with you that change is needed; but because of the tenuous nature of their authority and the intensity of their obligations to their faction, they cannot personally be the champion of change. They will support you behind the scenes and help you navigate the political terrain, but they cannot be expected to be the public face of change, at least not until there is a tipping point and enough people think doing so is a good idea.

Every now and then, courageous boundary keepers show up who, by virtue of monitoring the group's boundaries and watching for danger, not only see the urgent need for change but also are willing to be the champions of change. They take on this challenge at great personal risk. Your task as a change agent is to work with these boundary keepers to ensure that the disruptions are not excessive and that the message is clear and appropriate for their faction. Sometimes, in the eagerness to push forward, a change agent does not appreciate the constraints and dangers for boundary keepers and expects them to do too much too soon.

Some boundary keepers will never support you. If the boundary keepers are resistant, recalcitrant, and outright obstructionist, then you should consider going around them directly to the people. In going directly to the people, you get to make your case without it being filtered or distorted by the boundary keeper. You get to explain the problem as you see it and the reasons for change. And you may also find people on the front lines who share your concern, want to do something about it, and are willing to join you in exercising leadership from their vantage point.

Dr. Robert Coles and his colleagues used this approach in mobilizing otherwise-resistant people to address serious child malnutrition in the South. Rather than have the change process be perceived exclusively as an elitist, top-down process being advocated by outsiders, they identified and worked with grassroots organizations such as community groups, pediatricians, committed local politicians, and religious organizations to be the bearers of the message and the champions of change. These groups, with support from Senator Kennedy, Coles, and others, were able to work the issues at the local level and put pressure on their political boundary keepers in the state and federal governments to support the work of change, ultimately making considerable progress in addressing the problem.

Even the least ugly change agents who respectfully and effectively leverage boundary keepers can still run into challenges that will not budge. In those cases, crossing borders may not be enough, and the deliberate busting of boundaries may be required. The next chapter describes how.

CROSSING BOUNDARIES
QUESTIONS FOR PRACTICE

1. What boundaries need to be crossed to mobilize people to tackle the interdependent challenge?

2. What are the diverse group cultural narratives you can expect to encounter?

3. How might you intervene to make it their work and not yours, ensuring that you do not become overly responsible for fixing the problem and turning your mission into a crusade?

4. Which groups may need to suffer losses in pursuing adaptive change, and how might you help them sustain their losses to make a successful transition?

5. Who can be your boundary-crossing partners? How can they help you navigate the terrain and compensate for your blind spots and biases?

6. How might you manage the perception of ugliness that others might project onto you?

7. Who are the boundary keepers, and what threat do you represent to them? How might you enroll the boundary keepers?

CHAPTER 4

Busting Boundaries

Breaking Up Maladaptive Practices

S ometimes the work of leadership requires busting the boundaries of your own group to free up the system to better respond
to both internal and external challenges that threaten the
group. Busting boundaries is about breaking up a set of maladaptive
practices and mindsets that hinder people's capacity to deal with
reality. These set of practices create a psychological, emotional, or
cultural boundary for the group, informing what people believe
they should or should not do in order to survive. When the practices
are maladaptive, boundaries need to be busted, or else danger
awaits and opportunities will pass people by. The persistence of
the group's maladaptive practices might also contribute to larger
systemic problems that in the long run endanger other groups

as well as themselves. Specifically, leadership to bust boundaries is needed when

- the group has flawed values, practices, and mindsets that reduce problem-solving capacity and impede progress;
- the group operates in a silo and is insular, parochial, and unwilling to open up its boundary to integrate greater complexity or cooperate with other groups to address an interdependent challenge; or
- the group, at great risk to itself, is avoiding facing the reality of changed conditions.

Maladaptive practices are an expression of the group cultural drift. All groups have habitual ways of operating and responding to predictable problems, and, given their cultural drift, they are inclined to neglect attending to significant shifts in their environment that necessitate changes in some of their values, habits, practices, and priorities. In fact, any human system is in danger of some kind of loss, breakdown, or even collapse if it cannot correct itself fast enough when dealing with an unfamiliar threat or changed conditions.

In *Collapse: How Societies Choose to Succeed or Fail*, social scientist Jared Diamond relates the fascinating example of the Viking community of Greenland that broke down about five hundred years ago. They came from their Scandinavian homeland in 1000 A.D. and settled on the large island that we know today as Greenland, where they built a robust community. Within a few hundred years, however, they disappeared. Why? Because they failed to face the reality that their lifestyle as manifest in their routine habits and practices was inconsistent with what was required to thrive in the environmental context of Greenland. They followed the traditions and approaches they had known in the old land, even though that lifestyle could not be sustained due to insufficient resources in the new land. They cut down the forests, overgrazed the land, and depleted the soil of essential nutrients. In the end, after fierce battles among themselves for control of the community and the few remaining resources, many died or starved to death, or simply abandoned the island in an attempt to find new territory or to return to the motherland. Their community collapsed.[1]

The Norse of Greenland lived within a relatively tight cultural boundary, which protected and perpetuated practices that eventually became maladaptive and contributed to their collapse. The collapse possibly could have been avoided. Had they noticed earlier the reality of their predicament and summoned the political will and leadership to take corrective action, they might have survived and succeeded. Had they opened up their cultural boundary and included the traditional people of the region, the Inuit, they could have learned new skills pertaining to kayak fishing, navigation of local waters, and survival strategies for a harsh environment. Because the Vikings were unwilling to open their boundaries to learn and to modify their values, habits, practices, and priorities, they perished.

Economic historian Niall Ferguson's research shows that many thriving nations and civilizations faded virtually overnight because they did not curtail the excesses of their maladaptive behaviors pertaining to economic practices. Collapse was not the result of a steady decline that occurred over centuries but, rather, the result of persistent bad habits or flawed assumptions that produced the illusion of progress when things were going well but proved disastrous when exposed to a sudden shock or new and complex realities.[2]

Even in the realm of modern business, breakdowns and collapse are a regular occurrence. Of the Fortune 500 companies in existence fifty years ago, only about 13 percent are around today.

Eighty-seven percent have disappeared through bankruptcy, merger, or simply closing shop.[3]

Consider the case of General Motors, one of America's leading automotive manufacturers. Due to foreign competition, burgeoning business costs, and internal cultural problems, the company collapsed in 2009 and filed for bankruptcy. The U.S. government decided to bail out the sinking company, believing the consequences for the economy would be too disastrous if GM failed. After the bailout, GM began rebuilding itself. It had many adaptive practices that could be used to promote growth, but it also had some maladaptive practices that were not diagnosed and fixed—particularly as it pertained to improving the quality of its vehicles. In 2013, another breakdown occurred: nearly 2.6 million vehicles were recalled because of a faulty ignition switch that was linked to accidents, injuries, and deaths.[4] The defective switch, which failed to release airbags during collisions, was the product of an internal cultural drift that did not value honest, open conversations or the generation of valid information that could be shared to address critical problems. GM management had heard for more than ten years from customers, dealers, the press, and their own ranks about the flaws with the ignition switch, but they continually neglected to take action.[5]

The new CEO, Mary Barra, told a congressional hearing on June 18, 2014, that an independent analysis had revealed that GM had serious cultural flaws, including organizational silos. This siloed behavior led groups not to share information, and the emergence of maladaptive practices arose included the "GM nod" and the "GM salute." The "nod" was used by managers to acknowledge agreement when a problem was brought up, but there would be no intention to follow through. The "salute" was a crossing of the arms followed by pointing outward, indicating responsibility lay elsewhere.[6] The cultural drift of blame and avoidance of responsibility threatened the company's credibility, profitability, and customer safety. Clearly, there was insufficient leadership at all levels of the organization to disrupt the prevailing cultural drift, call attention to the maladaptive practices and silos that had produced the errors, and bust counterproductive boundaries.

Groups refuse to bust maladaptive boundaries and practices and end up breaking down because (1) they are apathetic, complacent, or arrogant and do not want to change, (2) they do not see how their local behavior connects with the behavior of others to generate a systemic breakdown, (3) they see evidence of the problem but treat it as a technical or routine problem and provide the wrong response, or (4) they are unwilling to suffer the losses or to make the sacrifices needed to adjust to a new reality or changed condition.

Intervening to call attention to maladaptive practices and to bust constraining boundaries is not an easy task. As a change agent, you will encounter resistance and resentment for trying to alter the values and practices that the group considers essential for their survival and protection. Formal or informal boundary keepers might also seek to neutralize you because they see you as a threat to the group or to their personal status. Nevertheless, with sensitivity and smart strategy, you can make progress.

Provoke People to Face Reality

As a change agent, you must be an "attention manager." Attention is the essential resource for the promotion of change. To get people's attention you must find creative ways to engage others' interest and to point the spotlight on a problem long enough for people to see that there is a problem that demands their attention and to ignite a process of discovery and change. One way of getting attention is by provoking the group—shaking people out of their comfort zones to a state of discomfort.

The provocative intervention seeks to irritate or disturb the group. It is an agitation to the status quo. It seeks to disrupt that part of a person's thinking that is stubborn, stuck, dogmatic, and resistant.

Provoke by Asking Tough Questions

A tough and well-timed question can be a form of provocation. Rather than lead with the "answer," a well-crafted provocative question can get the group's attention, stimulate deep thinking, and spur action. It can interrupt the prevailing currents of the group cultural drift momentarily for the consideration of an issue that people have not considered or have been denying, avoiding, or simply missing because they are preoccupied with other concerns. Opportunities are abundant in meetings, forums, and informal gatherings to raise provocative questions and to challenge dogmatic beliefs, "sacred cows," and the logic of specific strategies or policies. In a meeting, you might ask, "Why are we really doing this?" "What are the assumptions underlying this policy or strategy?" or "Do you know what the consequences of persisting with this action could be?"

Provoke by Putting Hard Reality in Front of People

Sometimes the group needs more than a question to provoke thinking and action—it needs hard data. A provocative intervention could be putting a piece of hard reality in front of people that they would prefer to avoid. It might be letting them know that danger is at the door and the group will suffer great losses unless they change. It could be illustrating how their behavior is counterproductive and generating unintended and undesirable consequences. A corporate CEO, for example, might need to present the hard reality to the staff that new competitors are eating away at the company's market share, and unless a major cultural change occurs that increases productivity and sales, the company will not survive.

I once worked with a CEO of a large bank who did just this: he called his top one hundred managers together for an off-site meeting to present threats to the company—both internal and external—and to explore what changes were needed to take the company into the future. He wanted the managers to see that *they* were a major part of the problem and that it was their behavior that was impeding progress. Hierarchical, managerial, and professional boundaries contributed to counterproductive politics and slowed the pace of change. To set a personal example of the new openness and boundary busting needed to transform the organization, the CEO invited senior and midlevel executives to give him honest feedback on his leadership performance and his capacity to lead the company to future success. Anticipating the difficulty for people to speak openly in his presence, he left the room.

As the facilitator to this event, I was worried that the executives would resist the invitation. On the contrary, they saw this as an unprecedented opportunity and filled their flip charts with ideas on how the CEO could lead the bank better. When he returned, the CEO patiently listened to their feedback. When the executives had finished, he thanked them for their honesty and promised that he would seriously consider their recommendations. He then told them that a group of midlevel employees would now share their own feedback on the quality of the management being provided by the senior executives in the room! The midlevel staff, with a degree of trepidation, proceeded to deliver a scathing evaluation of the quality of the senior managers' leadership. In fact, they held them responsible for the bank's mediocre culture and all the dysfunctional political machinations that were paralyzing collaboration and innovation, perpetuating silos, and, ultimately, preventing positive change. The managers were shocked but also fascinated by the process. After seriously considering the data, they agreed that they, too, needed to change.

Provoke by Giving a Zen Slap

Provocation can also be in the form of a "Zen slap"—a strategically timed declaration (or even a spontaneous declaration) that something is wrong, broken, or needs to change. In the practice of Zen, the teacher hits the student at the right time to wake him up to the reality that he is distracted from meditation—that he is going in the wrong direction. It is not a punitive slap but a teaching slap that in effect says "Wake up—get focused and do the right thing." In the context of leadership, the Zen slap calls attention to people's ignorance, arrogance, hypocrisy, and the discrepancy between what people espouse and what they do. Its intention is not to embarrass or to humiliate, but to awaken people to focus on dealing with the maladaptive aspects and consequences of their behavior, and to appreciate that these practices need to be eliminated.

An example of a Zen slap is the intervention made in the national parliament by Australia's first female prime minister, Julia Gillard, in 2012 when she highlighted sexist behavior in politics. In a heated debate, she told the leader of the opposition, "I will not be lectured about sexism and misogyny by this man. Not now, not ever. The leader of the opposition says that people who hold sexist views and who are misogynists are not appropriate for high office. Well, I hope the leader of the opposition has got a piece of paper and is writing out his resignation."[7] Gillard was angry with him for making what she interpreted as sexist remarks about her, as many other men in politics, public forums, and the media had done.

Gillard's Zen slap was a provocative intervention that had a powerful impact on both Australia and other countries, generating front-page headlines throughout the week. It reignited an important debate in society around sexism, gender boundaries, and public leadership. One female observer noted, "I almost had shivers down my spine, I was so relieved that she had actually named what was happening. She was so angry, so coherent and able to register that enough is enough."[8]

The Zen slap is a risky intervention. Someone might slap you back! But in the right context and when skillfully executed, it can put the spotlight on the problem in a way that few other forms of intervention can do—by disrupting the prevailing cultural drift and shaking people out of their complacency to begin addressing maladaptive behaviors they have come to accept, tolerate, or even promote.

As explained, there are many different ways to perturb and provoke a group. You can make demands; call attention to people's neglect, duplicity, or hypocrisy; raise an issue that no one wants to discuss; stand firm on a principle; ask a tough question; challenge a group assumption; or put a piece of reality directly in front of people that gets them to face what have been reluctant to face. Ultimately, if your provocation is successful, it will help people learn something about themselves and the problem that they had not appreciated before, and take the first steps toward change.

You should anticipate the possibility that your provocative intervention will generate conflict within the group. Conflict through the passionate presentation and exploration of competing perspectives is an important feature of adaptive work. Therefore, as an attention manager, you must adjust the intensity of your provocation according to people's readiness to learn and capacity to handle conflict. If you are too provocative, they might flee from responsibility for engaging in the adaptive work of change, or they might attack you or other groups that they perceive as a threat to their boundaries or habitual practices. However, if you are not provocative enough, you may not get attention at all, nor will there be sufficient heat to spark a learning process.

Evoke the Noble Sentiments of People to Do the Right Thing

Not all interventions need to be provocative. You might use a combination of provocative and evocative interventions if you are to be effective. While the provocative intervention agitates the group to stir action, the evocative intervention appeals to higher values and noble sentiments. It seeks to engage that part of the person's thinking that is willing, open, imaginative, and can see potential. The word *evoke* means "to bring forth"; thus, the evocative intervention—through education, inspiration, and invitation—seeks to bring forth, elicit, or draw out from people values, thoughts, and feelings that transcend self-interest and tribalizing instincts, and include the courage to bust boundaries, suffer losses, and be responsible for the creative work of change.

The noble values, virtues, and sentiments of people are sometimes latent, waiting to be ignited and expressed. Often other concerns such as the need for personal advancement, honoring group loyalties, the hunger for immediate gratification, an abiding cynicism, and reality of daily survival needs override the values of acting on our noble virtues. Therefore, your task is to perturb people into action by evoking feelings and thoughts that lead people to conclude that the work of change is worth pursuing.

Many people are open to change, but they need a reason to do it or at least the feeling in their hearts that it should be done. Not only do they need a reason and a feeling, they often need some encouraging support and a nudge to move them in the right direction. A way to evoke the noble sentiments of people is through the power of story.

Evoke Through the Power of Story

When you show up to provide leadership, people will wonder what you are doing and why are you doing it. They will start analyzing you and your motivations. You need a story to shift the attention from you to the adaptive challenge.

From the beginning of time, stories have been important to individuals and their communities in helping people deal with sudden disruptions in their life and the consequent need for change. The great holy books of all religions are a collection of stories carefully crafted to illustrate important precepts and values that help people make sense of the human experience and navigate the complexities and dangers of a bewildering world.

Stories give life to the work of change and make it real and personal. They bring a human dimension to the problem, allowing people to see elements of themselves in the story and also the humanity of others. They generate images in the mind—conceptualizations and interpretations—that move people to action in ways that the straightforward presentation of facts, statistics, bureaucratic directives, or hierarchical commands can never achieve. A well-told story generates an opening, a clearing in the fog, for a moment at least, that leaves people interpreting and relating to the challenge differently from how they did before.

The power of a story lies in generating a human connection to the challenge so that people want to learn more about the problem or start doing something to address it. Chatrini Weeratunge used the power of story to get a Sri Lankan garment manufacturer with more than fifty thousand employees, mostly women, to do the right thing and support comprehensive intervention to address violence against women and sexual harrassment—insidious practices that were widespread in the larger community.

She approached the top executives and explained the problem, but they showed little interest, telling her, "We are not an NGO." She left the meeting despondent but decided to try again, this time with a more compelling story. She realized that they did not understand the nature of the problem and she had to tell the story differently. "They saw me as a do-gooder, and I saw them as heartless corporate types, which didn't help. I went back to them and told the story in a way that made sense to them. I used the language of business and talked about how the abuse of these women impacted their performance and the productivity of the company; and if they wanted better results and a more satisfied and motivated workforce, they should support the empowerment of women." This time the company agreed, leading to one of the most innovative programs in the country.

My colleague at Harvard, Marshall Ganz, is one of the foremost authorities on mobilizing people through the power of story—in particular, three critical stories: the story of self, the story of us, and the story of now. His framework has informed my own thinking of the strategic value of story in getting attention and mobilizing action.

In Chapter 2 on diagnosis, I explained that groups already have powerful narratives that define who they are and how they think about problems. These stories generate a cultural drift, a patterned way of behaving that requires little questioning or thought and allows the group to drift through life. The challenge of leadership in evoking positive engagement through telling a story is to ensure that (1) the story makes the issue interesting, relevant, accessible, and makes sense to people in the context of their own group narrative, and (2) the story is told in a way that perturbs the prevailing group narrative and prods people to think in new ways about the challenge beyond what the group's cultural narrative currently allows for.

Generally people do nothing about a problem because they do not know enough about the problem, do not care enough about the problem, or feel they cannot do anything to solve the problem. The challenge in telling a story is to leave people feeling that they now know something about the problem, should care about the problem, and can actually do something about it. The story should be educational, aspirational, inspirational, and invitational. Let me explain.

First, the story of change should be educational and informative. The story should put the reality of the problem in front of people. Reality is hard-edged, and you want people to feel that edge. A well-told story can serve to paint a graphic image that causes people to sense that the problem is real and serious and that change is needed. What might be the consequences if this challenge is not addressed promptly? What will the group lose?

Adaptive, boundary-busting work is a disruption to the lives of people. It necessitates sacrifice, loss, and a degree of painful adjustment. Your story of change should speak to the reality of what the journey might be like, the bewilderment that can be expected, and the possible joy and gains if the work succeeds.

Second, the story of change should be aspirational. It should be on behalf of a higher purpose. It explains what progress might look like and what it means for things to get better. You should include powerful imagery. What image in the people's minds might help them overcome their reluctance and make a commitment to the work of change? The evocative image must be powerful enough to make people feel that the time, attention, and resources they will be called to expend are worth the sacrifice. If the imagined state is weak or inadequate, the people might feel no compelling reason to tackle the change and quickly revert to the security of their boundaries, habit, and custom.

Third, the story of change should be inspirational. *Inspire* means to "breathe life" into people. In a world filled with cynicism and despair, where few things live up to their promise, inspiration is needed to draw out the fragile, suppressed elements and sentiments of a group in order to get people to do the right thing, be more responsible, and pursue mutually beneficial change.

Rather than think of inspiration as the product of charisma, think of it as a poetic act. I do not mean that you should literally speak poetry, but you should use words, imagery, symbols, and allegories to shift people's relationship to the problem. Poetic speaking triggers the imagination and helps people to transcend the confines of their current understanding. Great poetry has a way of bringing light to darkness and allowing people to see and feel things that give profundity to the moment and provide the possibility of change. In Shakespeare's *A Midsummer Night's Dream*, Theseus says:

> The lunatic, the lover, and the poet are of imagination all compact:
> One sees more devils than vast Hell can hold, this is the madman;
> The lover, all as frantic, sees Helen's beauty in the brow of Egypt.
> The poet's eye, in a fine frenzy rolling, doth glance from heaven
> to earth, from earth to heaven; And as imagination bodies forth
> the forms of the things unknown, the poet's pen turns them to
> shapes and gives to airy nothing a local habitation and a name.[10]

There are perhaps a lot of lunatics and lovers masquerading as change agents through the brilliance of their poetic prowess and their ability to talk about "airy nothing," but the true change agent must harness and use the power of poetic inspiration to give "airy nothing" or the abstract nature of change "a local habitation and a name." They must seek to ground it while allowing for the imagination, beauty, and mystery of the process.[11]

Finally, the story of change should be invitational. You need to explain to people what engaging in adaptive work might look like—what will be involved, what might happen, and who needs to do what. The story presents an invitation to partner in the work with a sense of urgency. If people do not appreciate what is at stake and the urgency of the challenge, they will be inclined to delay their involvement.

The request for action must be consistent with what the people are ready for and are capable of. If the request is too extreme, the people will reject it. If the request is too little, the people might think the problem is not that serious. However, it is important to let people know that small things can make a big difference. Sometimes change seems overwhelming and very distant, but if people can appreciate that they can do small tasks immediately that can make a visible and practical difference, then their attention will be piqued.

In presenting the story of change, you must appreciate that some people will resonate to the story more than others. Some people will say, "I agree—we must change"; some people will remain skeptical and say, "Well, I really don't want to change"; and still others will be outright opponents who believe, "We must stop this change." But there will also be people who step forth and say, "I want to play a more active leadership role in the orchestration of change." These people can become your network of change agents, the topic of the next section.

Develop a Network of Internal Change Agents

You should not attempt to bust the boundaries of the group alone. It is too risky. To promote adaptive work, you need to build a network of change agents who can do the provoking and evoking that you alone cannot do. They can speak to the specific concerns and fears of their respective factions. Change is a disruption, even a threat, to the prevailing cultural drift and the narratives and values that people cherish. Not everyone will want to change, and some factions will need more time and attention than others. A network of change agents helps you to anticipate and make sense of the kinds of resistance that will inevitably emerge, they help groups sustain and manage the inevitable losses that accompany change, and they are able to develop contextually appropriate strategies to address the specific concerns of each group.

Change of any sort is a gamble, and there can be no guarantee of success. In the social science literature, system justification theory argues that people are often motivated to defend and legitimize the systems in which they work or live, even if those systems are unfair, undesirable, or ridden with serious problems.[12] This tendency is stronger in people who depend on the current system for their survival or feel that they cannot do much to change the current system. If people derive some benefit from the current system, they might be less inclined to want to tinker with it. If they feel that they cannot do much to change the present conditions, when that system is being challenged, they might actually be motivated to defend and justify the system or even view it in a more favorable light, believing that it is really not so bad.[13] A network of change agents can work with their respective factions and speak the story of change in a way that connects to people's aspiration for a better future while also acknowledging people's resistance is often a product of the fear of what they must lose or sacrifice.

A network of internal change agents was used to orchestrate Japan's Meiji Restoration in the latter part of the nineteenth century that led to one of the most significant transformations in education, governance, technology, and infrastructure that the world has seen.[14] This network included samurai, administrators, scholars, and merchants, as well as more than three thousand Westerners brought to Japan to share their expertise. Hundreds of Japanese change agents also traveled to foreign countries to observe and learn from people experienced in addressing similar problems and leading change; and when they returned to Japan, they joined the internal network of change agents that would lead the reforms.

While the change agents during the Meiji period were mostly former lords, samurai, and educators, some were also amazing women who provided courageous leadership to address the superstitions and narratives pertaining to the role of women in Japanese society. One of these change agents was Toshiko Kishida, a tutor to the empress in the Imperial court. She eventually left the court, considering it "far removed from the real world" and a "symbol of the concubine system that was an outrage to women."[15] She felt strongly that women needed to play a greater role in Japan's modernization process. She wrote, "We are trying through a cooperative effort to build a new society . . . yet in this country, as in the past, men continue to be respected as masters and husbands while women are held in contempt as maids or serving women. There can be no equality in such an environment."[16] One of her famous statements is "If it is true that men are better than women because they are stronger, why aren't our sumo wrestlers in the government?"[17]

Kishida devoted herself full-time to gender reform. She traveled the country giving a talk she called "Maidens in Boxes." The speech highlighted three boxes, or boundaries, that constrained girls' development, and she advocated that these boundaries be busted. The first box pertained to the way parents kept their daughters in the home and did not allow them to be exposed to outside influences. The second box pertained to the way in which parents demanded absolute obedience from their daughters and constrained the opportunities for choice and self-expression. The third box pertained to the lack of educational opportunities for girls. In her speech, Kishida criticized parents for the harm they do to their daughters, but at the same time she acknowledged that the harm was not intentional but the result of their desire to see their daughters fit into a particular role in the context of the prevailing cultural traditions. She advocated free choice for girls "to tread wherever their feet might lead and stretch their arms as wide as they wished." But she also said that the breaking of the boxes should be done at a steady pace, because if the boxes were busted too hastily, the daughters trapped in the boxes would probably run away![18]

Although she was fined and once imprisoned for her views, Toshiko Kishida's work proved instrumental in triggering Japan's "first wave" of feminism, busting some key gender boundaries that existed at the time, and contributing to the success of the Meiji reforms.[19] She was a part of the network of multiple change agents, working reform at different levels of society to expedite and deepen change throughout the nation.

Your network of change agents need to be encouraged, supported, and protected. They will be an irritant to some factions because they will be challenging the prevailing order, and therefore boundary keepers might emerge to neutralize them. If they are isolated and alone, then their neutralization will go unnoticed.

However, if there is a network, people can assist one another and ensure protection is given and guidance provided on how provocative or evocative they need to be and how to navigate the social, cultural, and political space.

If Boundary Keepers Block Progress, Start a Movement

When maladaptive practices are pervasive, entrenched, or protected by an elite and powerful group of boundary keepers, one way to tackle the problems is by creating a movement. A movement is an informal network of people who coalesce around a shared aspiration or problem. By virtue of the group's interest in and excitement about that aspiration, a certain buzz emerges and momentum develops that makes it hard for others to ignore. A powerful movement stands *for* something rather than being against something. An adaptive challenge is about bringing something new into existence. It is creative work that takes time. Therefore, the movement must unequivocally champion the higher purpose or noble aim. You must also manage the boundaries of the movement, or else anyone for any reason might jump on the bandwagon to promote their narrow agenda.

An example of someone who created a movement that perturbed a stubborn and complacent group of boundary keepers that was blocking progress was the seventy-four-year-old social reformer Anna Hazare. The problem in India that Hazare wanted to highlight was rampant corruption at all levels of government, a problem that directly affected every Indian citizen. Hesitant to do the right thing, the government dragged its feet in enacting tougher anti-corruption laws.

In the spirit of Gandhi, to spotlight the problem, and to harness the discontent of ordinary people, Hazare began a public hunger strike on April 5, 2011, and invited people to join him in protest. So confident was the government in its ability to preserve the status quo, officials arrested him in front of national and international television cameras and journalists—as Hazare expected.

The images of a defensive government using a heavy-handed approach on an old man who was calling attention to a legitimate problem was too much for most Indians to take. Hazare's hunger strike, followed by his public arrest, ignited people's noble senti-ments to take a stand for a corruption-free government and led tens of thousands all across India to join Hazare in further protest. After five days, the government accepted Hazare's demands and issued a declaration that a joint committee of government and civil society representatives would convene to draft new legislation addressing corruption, thus advancing the adaptive challenge of generating good governance across India, one step further.[20]

Sometimes the boundary keepers are so dysfunctional and detrimental that the movement must actually work to remove them. This is an extreme measure, but in some circumstances it might be needed. Srđja Popović of Serbia came to this conclu-sion—along with the majority of Serbian citizens—in deciding that it was time to topple the president, Slobodan Milošević.[21] The question was, How? Popović was a young biologist studying at university when he and his friends created a civic youth movement called Otpor! in 1998. His group, embodying the sentiment of the nation, was tired of the authoritarian government, as it had mismanaged resources, stoked old ethnic tensions, violated human rights, started three wars and was about to launch a fourth with Kosovo, and was clearly an impediment to democratic reform and national progress. In 2000, by virtue of Otpor!'s unrelenting campaign, Milošević could see that he did not have the support of the people and that it was futile to hold on to power any longer, so he resigned. In 2001, he was arrested and tried for international war crimes in The Hague. He died in prison in 2006.

How did Popović do it? He harnessed the discontent of ordinary people and channeled it into a movement. He used that movement to generate interventions that spotlighted the contradiction between people's aspirations and Milošević's behavior. He made the movement fun and interesting. He got students out into the streets and also mothers and the elderly banging pots and pans at designated times—sending a loud, clear message to Milošević that he had to change, or he had to go.

Not all movements need to threaten the boundary keepers or remove them altogether. Sometimes boundaries can be busted by generating a movement of ideas that leads the boundary keepers to realize that they and the larger system must change. That was true for IBM in the 1990s.

The IBM executives had essentially ignored the Internet and failed to see its potential. By analogy, IBM had bet all its money on perfecting buggy whips, while the automobile was right around the corner.[22] The initial change agent who sought to wake up IBM to its flawed thinking was a young engineer named David Grossman. In 1994, he realized that IBM had not even begun to comprehend how the Internet could become an integral part of business. This realization came to him as he watched the winter Olympics in Norway via television and on the Internet. IBM, an official sponsor, was responsible for collecting and displaying the results of the games. Grossman noticed that the competitor Sun Microsystems was taking the IBM data and displaying it on its own website. Grossman said, "If I didn't know any better, I would have thought that the data was being provided by Sun. And IBM didn't have a clue as to what was happening on the open Internet." When he spoke to his colleagues, Grossman was surprised by their ignorance. He subsequently took a workstation with him and drove to IBM headquarters four hours away at Armonk, New York, to personally meet with a group of senior executives and get them to see what was happening on the Web and to appreciate how IBM was missing a tremendous opportunity. While the executives found his presentation interesting, they did not share his excitement.

One of the executives, John Patrick, did see the potential in what Grossman was advocating. The two men continued the conversation and plotted their strategy for getting top management's attention. Patrick knew that management would not be open to Grossman's ideas unless there was more compelling evidence. So rather than work from the top down, they decided to create a movement. They started a grassroots campaign by getting interested employees to create a "Web community" that would conduct experiments, share ideas, and learn from one another about the realities and possibilities of the Internet in IBM's future. Within a short time, their movement had hundreds of members and infiltrated all corners of the company. Lou Gerstner, IBM's new chairman, heard about the movement and was fascinated—and the rest is history. The company succeeded in creating a vision of opportunities that revolutionized the way in which IBM does business, turning the computer manufacturer into a global service provider that focuses on e-business and the Internet.

Contain People's Anxiety and Mischief

When a boundary is busted and a habitual way of operating comes to an end, people might either break free and create, or break-down and destroy. When people are excessively stressed they might reject change—not because they do not value change but because they suffer loss—the loss of status, competence, and familiar ways—and experience feelings of confusion, uncertainty, and incompetence. Boundaries are needed for safety and order, and when familiar and treasured boundaries disappear people can easily become distressed. Therefore, as a general principle, you do not want to bust too many boundaries at a time, particularly boundaries that hold the group's sacred narratives and cherished practices.

When busting a boundary or breaking up a maladaptive practice, you must take responsibility for managing the group transition and pacing the work of change. If you do not manage this transition and contain people's anxiety and even mischief, the gains achieved by busting critical boundaries might be jeopardized.

Think for a moment about what happened in the Soviet Union when Premier Mikhail Gorbachev, from 1985 to 1991, busted two significant boundaries for his nation concurrently—perestroika, the economic boundary, and glasnost, the political boundary. Perestroika was the policy of economic liberalization that led to the sale of state assets and the embrace of free market capitalism. The process happened too fast—people did not have ample time to adjust. Resources were sold for cheap, given away, or simply taken. A few people became millionaires overnight, some became billionaires, and the Russian mafia cunningly exploited the economic chaos to their advantage. Glasnost was about political liberalization and openness; people could now form political parties and criticize the state. But as the country became overwhelmed by reports about burgeoning criminality as well as revelations of state crimes of the past, people lost confidence in the state's ability to lead them to the promised land of prosperity, or at least to stop society's descent into chaos.

Gorbachev, and his successor Boris Yeltsin, busted the boundaries that held the foundational narratives of the Soviet Union.

While fractures and maladaptive practices pervaded the economic and political system and that situation necessitated reformative change, many experts have argued that change happened too fast, was poorly managed, benefits were not dispersed, and some groups suffered greater losses than others, thereby unleashing anxiety and resentment.[23]

In contrast, China in the 1980s and 1990s took a more cautious approach to the work of reform. The Chinese steadily busted their economic boundary and freed up the system so that its citizens could participate in and enjoy the benefits of the global economy. It was an orderly transition orchestrated through the leadership of Deng Xiaoping.[24] He regulated the amount of disequilibrium the nation could tolerate. He knew that many of the old boundary keepers who had made the Long March with Mao were hard-core communists, anti-West, and vehemently against free market policies. The key to Deng's success was in conducting experiments in parts of the country by creating Special Economic Zones that allowed people to discover through trial and error what would work in China's unique context to generate prosperity for people, thereby building a readiness over time for system-wide reform. Today, China is an economic powerhouse, and hundreds of millions of people have transcended poverty because of Deng's paced and wise strategy.

In Chapter 3 on crossing boundaries, I presented the case of the powerhouse change agent Michelle Rhee and her attempt to reform an ailing school district. Rhee not only had to cross boundaries to mobilize people and resources; she also had to bust boundaries to fix maladaptive practices in the system. Administrative boundaries had to be busted so that the Central Office could work as a support service to schools rather than as a bureaucratic control center. The boundaries that kept teachers isolated in a classroom and not learning from other teachers and professionals needed to change in order to enhance instructional competence. The boundaries that kept parents at a distance and disengaged needed to be busted so that they could be included in the network of support for their children's learning. The boundaries of the teachers' union that protected the interests of teachers as an exclusive in-group needed to be busted to give principals a greater say in the promotion of a meritocratic system that encouraged and rewarded good teaching and innovation.

No one can doubt the nobility of Rhee's aspiration and commitment to the work of change. However, a major reason she was fired was because she busted too many boundaries and overwhelmed the system, and tried to do that work alone. A teacher wrote to Rhee saying, "There are too many initiatives going on. I'm worn out and overwhelmed. What's your priority?" Rhee responded by saying, "I hear you. In our exuberance to fix everything all at once, we've thrown so many different programs at you. Please know that this comes from a desire to support you, not inundate you. But I now see that we may have pushed on too many different fronts all at the same time."[25]

There might be times, given the sense of urgency and the dangers on the horizon, the challenge will be to expedite the process of change by launching a full-scale frontal assault by pushing on different fronts, busting many boundaries, and overwhelming people with programs, moral arguments, campaigns, and even threats in order to get people to change their ways and transform the system. This is a high-risk strategy, and few leaders do it well without generating considerable resistance, casualties, and mayhem. As a change agent, you cannot afford to be insensitive to the struggle of people to adjust to changed circumstances, sustain their losses, and find new ways of navigating and surviving in unfamiliar territory. You can be demanding, but you must also be compassionate and strategic.

To contain the anxiety and mischief, you will need a strong holding environment. A holding environment is like a container that holds the emotions, conflicts, and frustrations that accompany change. It allows—even encourages—people to wrestle with tough questions, hard facts, and value trade-offs. It helps in regulating the amount and intensity of change.

You must give serious thought to the ingredients and features of your holding environment. What should the role of authority be? How should the boundaries be managed? What symbols, ceremonies, and practices should be deployed to orient people? Attending to and managing the holding environment will be critical to your success.

BUSTING BOUNDARIES
QUESTIONS FOR PRACTICE

1. What are the group's maladaptive practices and impeding boundaries? Why do they persist?

2. How might you perturb the group cultural drift to generate attention on the problem?

3. What provocative interventions could you make to get people to face reality?

4. What evocative interventions might you make to draw out noble sentiments and get people to do the right thing?

5. How might you craft a story of change?

6. Do you have a network of change agents to broaden and deepen the work of change?

7. Who are the boundary keepers or resistant groups, and how might they block progress? How might you engage them? Do you need to start a movement?

8. How might you contain the anxiety and mischief of people that can happen when familiar boundaries are busted? What kind of a holding environment do you need?

CHAPTER 5

Transcending Boundaries

Promoting Creative Problem Solving

Boundary-transcending work is a process of exploration, experimentation, and adventure—without any guarantee of success but the possibility of remarkable accomplishment. As the NASA website declares, "Humans are driven to explore the unknown, discover new worlds, push the boundaries of our scientific and technical limits, and then push further."[1] This instinctual urge has generated, and will continue to generate, amazing innovations that produce advantage for all—but it will require leadership, even if that leadership is nothing more than encouraging people to take a step into the unknown.

Tolkien's epic stories *The Lord of the Rings* and *The Hobbit* illustrate the challenge. As the wiser and experienced hobbit Bilbo Baggins says to the younger Frodo, "It's a dangerous business going out your door. You step onto the road, and if you don't keep your feet, there's no knowing where you might be swept off to."[2] Such is the adventurous work of transcending boundaries—you do not know where you might be swept off to!

Many boundaries today become barriers to discovering critical information needed for survival, addressing multifaceted problems, and responding to new realities. The work in providing leadership is to transcend the confining boundary by stimulating the creative process and thus helping the group discover something new—a solution to an intractable problem, an invention, or a way of living and working together. Specifically, boundary-transcending work is needed when

- the group has exhausted its repertoire of problem-solving strategies and must now go into creative mode and innovate; or
- danger is at the door, and the group must leave treasured boundaries and explore uncharted territory to make a discovery or do something that it has never done before.

For example, boundary-transcending work in the form of radical innovation might be needed if a company must invent a new product, such as Apple did in creating an array of groundbreaking products under Steve Jobs's creative leadership. The task of the change agent leader is to stimulate sufficient imagination and courage so that the group can transcend the boundaries of habit and thinking, and produce a breakthrough result to the challenge that it is facing.

By its very nature, boundary-transcending adaptive work has the potential to be a transformative experience. In a dire situation where urgency is needed, it can make the difference between life and death. It is also demanding and precarious work, as sustaining the creative, exploratory state requires the willingness to challenge prevailing beliefs, tolerate conflict, and seriously consider unconventional notions that might be threatening to some. While boundary-transcending work is difficult, and emotionally and mentally demanding, it can also be exhilarating since it requires the playful exploration of ideas and a willingness to be deliberately outrageous and oftentimes unreasonable.

Hiroshi Mikitani: Transcending Boundaries at Rakuten

Hiroshi Mikitani is a boundary-transcending change agent and the founder and CEO of Rakuten, an e-commerce and Internet company headquartered in Tokyo, Japan. Mikitani has been transcending boundaries for most of his life. When he was thirty years old, he left a comfortable and secure job in a Japanese bank to start Rakuten, a courageous act for a young Japanese man.

Rakuten grew rapidly and within ten years had more than seven thousand employees. Although it developed a global reach, it remained fundamentally a Japanese company in culture and practice. The Japanese cultural drift, while having many strengths and advantages, also had limitations. Mikitani felt it was excessively group oriented and stifled creativity and entrepreneurial pursuits. People were generally cautious and risk averse. To encourage boundary-transcending creativity and the development of a global mindset, Mikitani did something radical: he made English the official working language of the company, even for all Japanese employees. "I launched it to disrupt a doomed process and replace it with a faster, more global, and more borderless functionality," he explained.[3]

Many critics believed that Mikitani was promoting English at the expense of the native tongue, but he was undeterred.[4] He felt that English had fewer power markers—words that specifically denote status and hierarchy—and could thereby facilitate problem solving faster, without the restraints of the Japanese cultural norms that get played out in language.

> When I insisted that everyone learn to communicate in English, I put them all on the path to thinking outside the boundaries of Japanese language. When you open your mind to another language, you open your intellectual experience to other cultures, to other ways of doing business. When you can use language to connect across borders, you can communicate on a new level with a wider range of people. . . . It frees you from whatever constraints your native language may have and empowers you to make global connections and learn from other traditions.[5]

Mikitani's leadership exemplifies one aspect of getting a group to transcend its boundaries in order to facilitate the challenge of becoming a global company. In Rakuten, people needed to transcend language, mental, and cultural boundaries in order to become more creative and generate a global business. His role was to create the space that allowed people to become more experimental to discover new ways of communicating and innovating—and so far his leadership has contributed to promising results. In 2014, *Forbes* listed Rakuten in the top twenty of the world's most innovative companies.[6]

Prepare People for the Adventure

In providing leadership to get people to transcend boundaries, you need to prepare them for the adventure. The challenge will require going beyond the safety and confines of secure boundaries to explore new frontiers of knowledge, action, and human experience. It is about venturing into the great unknown and making rapid shifts in direction as new discoveries about the terrain emerge. Transcending boundaries is a risky undertaking with an uncertain outcome and no guarantee of success, but the adventure brings with it the possibility of an exciting breakthrough.

Not everyone is ready for creative work or will embrace the spirit of adventure—understandably so, because a bold adventure is often riddled with uncertainty and unpredictable surprises, and can even be perilous. The leadership challenge is to work with the group to help them see the potential value of transcending the boundary and engaging in creative work, while at the same time being honest with people about the possibility of loss or failure.

Paradoxically, failure is an ingredient that can lead to success. *Failure* is an ancient word that in Latin, *fallare*, means simply to fall or stumble.[7] In going into unchartered territory, you will likely fall and stumble. Each fall allows you to learn more about the terrain. If you are unwilling to fall and stumble, your learning will be limited, and you will never create or pursue an adventure that could generate a breakthrough.

The renowned natural artist Andy Goldsworthy personifies the creativity-unleashing power of failure. In the award-winning documentary *Rivers and Tides*, he is creating an artistic stone sculpture by stacking more than a hundred pieces of slate. At one point the stones collapse. An exasperated Goldsworthy says, "This is the fifth time that has happened. I obviously don't know the stone well enough. But each time I have come to know the stone a little bit better, and my knowledge has increased in proportion to my failures."[8] This mindset must be present in the change agent as well as the group: every failure reveals a little more about the problem, the context, the social system, and various actors connected to the problem. A failure, an error, or a breakdown simply means that one does not know the system well enough, and through failure the opportunity is there to learn a little more about the complexity of the problem. In other words, one's discoveries can increase in direct proportion to the extent that one fails and is willing to learn from the failure.

Great companies also understand this principle. Jeff Bezos, the founder and CEO of the famously successful online retailer Amazon.com, said "You have to have a willingness to repeatedly fail if you're going to experiment. For a certain kind of person, that is a very exciting, very motivating culture. So, we attract those kinds of people."[9]

Most people, however, given the power of their group cultural drift, do not like to fail because of the shame and possible blame associated with it. The late Harvard professor Chris Argyris found that many ambitious professionals, by virtue of being success oriented or preoccupied with looking good and impressing others, do not deal well with failure. They suffer from what he termed the "brittleness syndrome." When confronted with failure, rather than examine how they contributed to the breakdown or error that produced the failure, they cover up mistakes or attribute blame to others, thus distancing themselves from a learning opportunity.[10]

Leadership, therefore, is needed to reduce the propensity of individuals and groups to mask mistakes and attribute blame to others or external conditions when engaged in experimentation and creative work. When honesty and straight talk accompanies inevitable breakdowns or misadventures, adaptive learning can unfold with greater speed and responsiveness. You try something, it fails, you learn from the failure, and you immediately shift direction and try something else. That process repeats itself over and over again until the group makes a useful discovery.

Harness the Power of Diversity

Given the complexity of today's problems, transcending boundaries can be enhanced by bringing a diverse group of people together to participate in problem solving and creative exploration—whether it is a global project team that must produce a breakthrough product or service, or a diverse network of people in a community that must address an intractable problem. There is power in diversity if you can provide sufficient leadership to stimulate that power.

Introducing diversity disrupts the prevailing group drift so that new ideas can emerge and creativity can be activated. Diversity might include multicultural, multisectorial, or multidisciplinary voices. What is key is that people have the opportunity to be exposed to contradictory perspectives and a multitude of views, values, and narratives. Empirical studies have shown that diverse groups perceive problems presented to them in more unique ways than members of homogeneous groups, and, under certain conditions, can outperform homogenous groups.[11]

Many institutions are harnessing the advantages of diversity. For example, Stanford University has its d.school (the design school), an institute that promotes innovation through diversity of perspectives and active engagement with real-world problems. Students and faculty from across the entire campus—medicine, the humanities, management, the sciences, engineering, and education—come together to learn about creativity and to collaborate in project teams to generate breakthrough solutions for some of the most complex problems organizations and communities face. Too often professional knowledge and academic disciplines are compartmentalized and serve to generate experts who have deep domain knowledge but lack the breadth and capacity to transcend their boundary, work across disciplines, and learn and co-create with others. The d.school believes that in a complex, globalized world that demands radical innovation, problems cannot be solved from one point of view, and therefore the adaptive challenge is to integrate multiple points of view.[12]

The multinational technology company Intel is also harnessing the power of diversity for innovation. Its strategy is to bust silos to create new knowledge leading to breakthrough products. Although its business is highly technical, Intel believes that innovation cannot happen from a pure technological platform but must be infused with imagination, creativity, and diverse perspectives and experience. It even hired an anthropologist to work full-time in the company to help with the process. "We use stories from everywhere to open up the conversation," anthropologist Genevieve Bell explained, "not to provide answers but to bring opportunities to ask different questions."[13] Exposure to different questions leads to different and often unconsidered perspectives. It helps people to step out of the confines of their cultural or professional narratives and explore diverse narratives and interpretations of reality more deeply, thereby enhancing creativity and innovation.

The research on creativity by the psychologist Mihaly Csikszentmihalyi and others concurs that creative problem solving is not an individual process of brilliance but a social process of active engagement of diverse perspectives.[14] Boundary-transcending creativity may depend on a variety of opposing ideas being represented and integrated so new structures of thought and understanding can appear. Similarity breeds groupthink and redundant information. People become predictable and unsurprising, as when a group shares the same cultural narrative and is trapped in a rigid cultural drift. Therefore, whether to trigger a scientific breakthrough, a business innovation, or public policy that makes a difference, the challenge is getting enough people who see the problem differently to cross-fertilize their ideas, generating something greater than what any one faction could produce alone.

Harnessing the potential power of diversity, however, is not easy. People generally prefer their own kind and cherish their boundaries. Therefore, it requires leadership to prod the group, ignite imaginative processes, and sustain the adventure. Without guiding leadership, diversity will fail to generate new possibilities because each individual or group will engage in tribalizing behavior to advance their own interests at the expense of others—as we often see at one of the most diverse organizations on the planet, the United Nations.

Think Like an Alchemist—Experiment to Get the Right Mix of People

To maximize the chance of success in harnessing the power of diversity, you must think like an alchemist and experiment with different combinations to see which mix generates the most creative outcomes.

Alchemy was a discipline that captivated some of the greatest minds of the Renaissance. The alchemists were the forerunners of modern science, and even Sir Isaac Newton dabbled in the mysterious art. They conducted unusual experiments mixing different chemicals and concoctions in the pursuit of new compounds and knowledge. Occasionally things blew up, but every now and then their experiments generated a remarkable breakthrough, such as finding the secret ingredients in European porcelain, or discovering that disease was not caused by an imbalance of the four bodily humors, or fluids, but harmful external agents that attacked the body and could be treated with natural remedies. The alchemists even gained insights into the anatomy and function of the brain.[15] Their perseverance, imagination, and willingness to experiment using different ingredients illustrate how you need to go about harnessing the power of diversity.

The research on diversity reinforces the view that the people who do best in diverse groups are curious, flexible, and open to novel experiences. Such people generally are not threatened by difference but actually have positive regard for people who are different from themselves, and they welcome being exposed to the unfamiliar as an opportunity to learn. They are also less anxious in situations of urgency, high ambiguity, and complexity.[16]

As you think about the mix you need, consider unique perspectives that can add dynamism to the problem-solving process. For example, mixing Millennials who grew up with social media with baby boomers who have experience navigating organizational politics can be a potent, mutually beneficial mix. Ideological or factional diversity can also be a source of creativity. President Abraham Lincoln famously created a "Team of Rivals" by appointing his three biggest opponents to his cabinet.[17] Each powerful in his own right, these men had clashing ideologies, styles, and personalities. Lincoln sensed that by harnessing diversity in his cabinet, he could generate enough creativity and shared commitment to end slavery and the Civil War—and this approach succeeded. Managing his team of rivals, however, was riddled with tension, but Lincoln handled it well. As a "political alchemist," he knew the strengths and weaknesses that each man brought to the table. He encouraged them to present their perspectives openly with one another and engage in healthy debate, as rancorous as it was occasionally. And, even though members of his team sometimes were spiteful and attacked Lincoln for their own political advantage, he had the temperament to rise above the jabs without taking it personally, continuing to work with them for the greater good. He saw his role as to manage the problem-solving and political processes by orienting his team to the higher purpose and helping them to overcome their petty rivalries and political differences to focus on the larger adaptive challenges facing the nation.

Whether comfortable or ill at ease mixing among others different from themselves, people need a higher purpose in order to bond when there are otherwise few reasons to do so. The higher purpose is the unifying mission; it explains why boundary-transcending work is needed, and what is at stake if it fails. It helps people to transcend fault lines to address a common challenge.[18] People will tolerate a lot of the frustration, conflict, and uncertainty that accompanies working in a diverse group if they share a higher purpose or superordinate goal with others, irrespective of their differences.

Promote Surprise Encounters

You may not have a mighty team of rivals like Lincoln, but an important thing you can do is promote "surprise" encounters with diverse people, even rivals, that bring varied perspectives to the creative work. Surprise encounters are informal and impromptu interactions with people that happen, sometimes by design, but often unexpectedly. By virtue of the encounter, something gets sparked that can contribute to the creative process. In other words, surprise encounters have the potential to generate valuable surprises.

The social science literature calls these informal encounters "weak-tie" connections.[19] Weak-tie connections are people or groups that you generally have little to do with, but for the purpose of stimulating the imaginative capacities of the group, you seek out their opinions and engage their viewpoint. Research indicates that the more pockets of distinct and potentially diverse information that can be accessed, formally and informally, the greater the potential for creativity.[20] For instance, a positive link has been found between the number of weak-tie acquaintances and the creativity of scientists[21] and also of software engineers and designers in the high-tech industry.[22] In strong-tie groups, where people know each other well through regular interaction, perspectives can easily become predictable and redundant. The predictability of a strong-tie group may be broken up by encouraging members to pursue surprise encounters that can spark the consideration of the challenge in a different light.[23]

Surprise encounters can be difficult to develop in institutions where people remain siloed. For example, accountants might stay within the boundaries of the finance department; graphic designers within the art department; and so on. Ed Catmull, president of Walt Disney Animation and Pixar Animation studios, said, "In creative work like ours, those barriers are impediments to producing great work, and therefore we must do everything to tear them down." Even the office structure at Pixar was designed to promote surprise encounters and stimulate creativity. "Most buildings are designed for some functional purpose," Catmull explained, "but ours is structured to maximize inadvertent encounters. At the center is a large atrium, which contains the cafeteria, meeting rooms, bathrooms, and mailboxes. As a result, everyone has a strong reason to go there repeatedly during the course of the workday. It's hard to describe just how valuable the resulting chance encounters are."[24] The Pixar building was the brainchild of none other than Steve Jobs, who after leaving Apple became a part owner of Pixar. He personally designed it to promote surprise encounters as he knew that engagement of difference was vital to the creative process.

Your building may not be like Pixar's, but you can still get people intentionally going out of their way to talk to people they normally would not interact with. They should be encouraged to cross boundaries in order to transcend boundaries.

Use Conflict for Creative Gains

Sometimes people use diversity as an excuse for avoiding tough issues. They hide behind diversity, being excessively respectful of the other and not engaging differences of perspective. But when pursuing boundary-transcending creativity, a degree of conflict can be helpful. In exercising leadership, you should not run from conflict but use it, and even orchestrate it, particularly when a group is too complacent or rushes to an incomplete agreement. The conflict must be monitored and managed to ensure that it does not overwhelm people and cause them to fight or flee, or inadvertently ignite a metaphorical fire that "burns down the house," thereby bringing the project to a disastrous end. That requires sensing when to turn up the heat, and when to turn it down.

As a contributor to the design of more than one hundred styles of automobiles, Jerry Hirshberg, the former head of design at Nissan, affirms the value of diversity and conflict in creative work.

> Multiple disciplines in the same studio, fights over what radio stations to listen to, divergent perceptions of appropriate work hours, modes of dress, codes of behavior, even what was perceived as quality work . . . all of this I saw as a rich and yeasty opportunity for a kind of friction I wanted to turn into light rather than heat. The uneasiness in my stomach and the fireworks in my brain told me there was some vital connection between the abrasiveness itself and original thinking. If we could grasp this connection, we would be tapping into a vast reservoir of creative energy.[25]

Indeed, the vast reservoir of creative energy can be tapped by knowing how to manage conflict and friction to promote innovation. That requires knowing what the different kinds of conflict are, how they get generated, and how they should be approached.

There are basically three kinds of conflict that you need to monitor—task conflict, relational conflict, and process conflict.[26]

Task conflict pertains to disagreements about the nature of the problem and the strategies to be pursued to address the problem. It is the clash of knowledge, domains of specialization, and experience. When task conflict emerges, the change agent should not stifle it but encourage it—fanning the flames by getting people to explain their point of view, challenge the assumptions of others, and express disagreements in order to capitalize on the wealth of expertise, experience, and informational differences. You might ask people, "Why do you think that way?" "What's your logic?" "Can you explain your underlying assumption?" "What really concerns you about what she said?" These kinds of questions surface, clarify, and test people's diverse perspectives.

Relational conflict is the clash of styles, personalities, values, and cultures. Problem-solving and creative work is never a rational exercise but always takes place in a swirl of competing values and sentiments. Some degree of clash of values is needed to generate contrast and to appreciate what is at stake for each faction participating in boundary transcending creative work. However, if there is too much relational conflict it might impede collaboration and the sharing of perspectives, leaving people feeling hurt, offended, and misunderstood. The degree of trust among group members drops as a result. When trust levels are low, differences in style and approach can become irritating and bothersome, thwarting the creative process. The leadership challenge is to promote a culture of tolerance, curiosity, listening, and resilience. Otherwise, relational conflict can quickly deteriorate as people take sides and defend their own subgroups and factions out of honor, loyalty, or to protect their group narrative, irrespective of the facts of the situation. Therefore, potentially fracturing relational concerns need to be surfaced early, worked through, and reconciled so that people are reoriented and can direct their energies to the challenge at hand.

Process conflict is the clash of roles of the individual actors in the group, the unconscious group dynamics, and the formal and informal alliances and factions that generate group forces that take a group in unintentional and counterproductive directions. In any group, there will be unconscious group dynamics—interactions that lead to the excessive dependency on one or two individuals to do the bulk of the work, the avoidance of embarrassing topics, the dynamics that produce false consensus, and behaviors that unintentionally exclude or marginalize some voices. You cannot really "manage" a group as no one is completely in control because everyone, even the leader, is subject to group forces that shape their behavior and problem-solving process. What you can do, however, is monitor group processes and ensure that all voices are encouraged, respected, and included.

Marginalization and exclusion are common in groups. When a perspective is repeatedly ignored, trivialized, or dismissed, you might partner publicly with the marginalized individual or subfaction by creating space for their voice to be expressed and seriously considered. When you notice a person has had her opinion stifled by being continually interrupted or talked over, you might say to the group, "Let's hear Susan's take on this issue. Susan, what do you think?"

Another aspect of handling conflict pertains to encouraging dissenting voices—those people who have radically different perspectives on the challenge but given the power of the group cultural drift find great difficulty expressing their perspective. Expressing dissent does not mean their assessment is correct. It might be wrong. The leadership task is to encourage the expression of dissent to promote deeper exploration and reconsideration of the group's big assumption, particularly when you see the group making a definitive statement about what the problem is and what the "correct" solution should be. The challenge is also to protect the dissenting voice—just as you protect the marginalized voice—because some group members might seek to bully the dissenter into submission or punish the person for the audacity to question the dominant position or apparent group consensus.

Promote Play

Play is an integral part of boundary-transcending creative work— not frivolous play, but imaginative, improvisational, exploratory, experimental play. If you are too positional or rigid in your beliefs, you will find it difficult to play. If you cannot play, you cannot create. Play is a way to think beyond constraints and the confines of the group cultural drift. The great educator John Dewey said that those people who make a difference in the world "give their minds free play about a subject without asking too closely at every point for the advantage to be gained; exclusive preoccupation with matters of use and application so narrows the horizon as in the long run to defeat itself. It does not pay to tether one's thoughts to the post of use with too short a rope."[27] Dewey advocated not jumping into practical application prematurely but to take the time to play with ideas and explore the possibilities.

In appreciating the nature of playfulness as it pertains to leadership and change, I am intrigued by the eighteenth-century philosopher, poet, and dramatist Friedrich Schiller. According to Schiller, "Man is only fully a human being when he plays."[28]

Schiller lived during the French Revolution and wrote his most famous treatise, "Letters on the Aesthetic Education of Man," on the eve of the execution of King Louis XVI. He was a front-seat observer to the madness of the revolution and was sickened by what he witnessed. He felt that the revolution had failed to deliver on its promise, leaving in its wake terror, fear, abuse, and death. Schiller said it well: "A great moment has found a little people."[29] His "Letters" was an attempt to offer the "change agents" of the time a more complete way to think about the process of orchestrating boundary-transcending change.

What was missing in the French Revolution, Schiller felt, was the willingness to play. Play may seem like an unusual concept in the context of a bloody revolution, but it is important because, in any boundary-transcending context, it is the mediating factor between reason and emotion. The playful approach is liberating, experimental, and allows a group to step into that psychological space to do things for which there is no prior concept or prede- termined strategy. It is the space of imagination, improvisation, and exploration. Schiller believed that the revolutionaries, on the one hand, were too rational and became dogmatic about what needed to be done. The ordinary citizen, on the other hand, was too emotional, driven by anger with the elites and the need for revenge. This mix of rigid dogmatism and volatile emotion led to thousands of people being executed throughout the country. It was a bitter and ugly revolution, under the guise of great promise.

Play requires putting dogma, rules, and regulations to the side. Dogma pertains to the belief about the way things should be done. Its function is to generate a thick boundary or "no-go zone." Play, in contrast, is the willingness to go beyond boundaries to explore the frontier.

Artists know the value of play. They work at the frontier, and they work in the realm of imagination, beauty, and judgment.[30] Play unleashes the power of the imagination that allows people to transcend the immediacy of the predicament and to take in a broader and richer perspective in order to notice opportunities, patterns, dynamics, and resources that they had never seen or considered previously.

Play is also about beauty and aesthetics. In corporate contexts, people tend to think in procedural and measurable ways based on inputs, outcomes, and key performance indicators. Aesthetics, in contrast, is about the unmeasurable and the unexplainable, the sublime and the transcendent. Giving space to the question of beauty in the context of innovation and creativity was the brilliance and obsession of Steve Jobs. He understood the nature of beauty in contributing to the exceptional products that Apple created under his leadership.[31]

With the beauty and aesthetic components of imaginative play comes judgment. Judgment is about critical thinking and moral reasoning. It is about choice. Art is not random, arbitrary, or capricious. There is a design inherent in art. It occurs in the context of limitations—the limitations of the size of the canvas and diversity of the paints on the palette. As Van Gogh and other great artists have shown, it is precisely because of the limitations that extraordinary, boundary-transcending art emerges. For the change agent and the group, judgments must be made, but the criteria and assumptions underlying those judgments must constantly be examined. Judgment, as it pertains to leadership, requires being wary of quick fixes and simple answers. There will, however, be times when judgment must be exercised and answers, solutions, and strategies must be decided and agreed upon. But in the spirit of exploration and play, the wise change agent knows that these judgments are simply a tentative place to stand in order to hold the group long enough to rest and regenerate before the next round of exploratory play begins.

My colleague Doris Sommer, through her Harvard initiative Cultural Agents, documents how artistry can generate extraordinary breakthroughs in political, social, and cultural reform.[32] She introduced me to the amazing Antanas Mockus, a man who understood the power of the arts in helping people go beyond constraining boundaries in the context of a city.

The Creative Leadership of Antanas Mockus

Antanas Mockus was the president of the National University of Colombia and a professor of philosophy and mathematics when he decided to run for mayor of Bogotá in 1995—and won. When he came into office, Bogotá was a broken city. Drug lords and criminal gangs made life unbearable. It had one of the highest murder rates in the world, corruption was rampant, poverty was endemic, and despair was everywhere.[33]

Mockus sensed that approaching the role of mayor as a traditional politician would be insufficient in mobilizing people to tackle the challenges of civic engagement. The people were cynical about politicians, regarding them as part of the problem. So Mockus decided to try a different tack. He approached the work of change as an artist. He wanted to appeal to the minds *and* hearts of the people. Change, he knew, would be difficult and painful, but it could also be playful and infused with humor. Therefore, he invited people to participate in small acts that could make a big difference. He wanted to get people to be responsible by helping them see that there were many domains of social and cultural life that they could shape and influence.

For example, to deal with one of the biggest problems the city faced—crowded roads and crazy drivers—he deployed more than four hundred mimes to perform on the streets, entertaining pedestrians, slowing down the traffic, and making fun of traffic violators. It worked. People enjoyed seeing the mimes on the street, and soon a sense of calm came to the busy streets of Bogotá.

Another problem was that women were afraid to go out at night for fear of being harassed or abused. Mockus said it was unacceptable that women did not feel safe in their own city, so he put in place a women's night out, asking men to stay at home and take care of children so that women could enjoy the downtown area without fear of harassment by men. More than seventy thousand women took to the streets and had a delightful time.

Mockus also mobilized people to address the problems of violence and terrorism. He invented a "vaccine against violence" and created a campaign to empower people by asking them to engage in a symbolic exercise of drawing the face of someone who has hurt them or a member of their family on a balloon, and then to pop the balloon. His message was "Do not let these terrible people have any more control over you. Get them out of your life."

Mockus evoked change in other ways using artistic or creative interventions. When the city faced a water shortage, he appeared on television in his shower, and he turned off the water as he soaped and asked the people to do the same. In a matter of months, people were using 14 percent less water. To promote civil and caring behavior, he distributed more than 350,000 "thumbs up" and "thumbs down" cards to the community. He asked people to hold up the appropriate card when they saw positive or negative behavior in the street or at work. During a difficult budget period, he asked people to pay a voluntary 10 percent extra in taxes to ensure that all the critical government services would not suffer. Sixty-three thousand people accepted the invitation and paid the tax. In fact, there was a dramatic shift in people's attitude toward the city government, which in the past was seen as notoriously corrupt and inept but was now viewed in a positive light, resulting in a threefold increase in tax collection compared with the previous city government.

Many people mocked Mockus for his approach. But his creative strategies generated an upbeat and positive mood in the city—a city that had been under a cloud of fear and despair for the previous two decades. The homicide rate fell 70 percent and traffic fatalities dropped by 50 percent. The city came alive with concerts, performances, art, theater, and all manner of novel and exciting activities. He used the power of play to harness people's frustration and disapproval with current conditions and to put the spotlight on specific problems and make interventions that helped break the chains of cynicism and despair and evoked three critical sentiments: (1) a belief that life can and will get better; (2) the feeling that citizenship, service, and community matter; and (3) a sense of personal responsibility for change and improvement.

Protect the Creative Space

Creative work generates conflict and anxiety, particularly as the group moves into "forbidden territory." The change agent must be able to hold that space to keep the creative and exploratory work alive long enough for discoveries to be made. Holding the space means protecting and promoting the creative process, particularly when group dynamics seek to smother creativity, smash that space, and cause the group to want to retreat from the adventure.

Creativity is the production of something new, and the process is typically not natural for a group. In fact, people usually get scared when doing real boundary-transcending exploratory work. It is very difficult to stand in the pain of unknowing. Something genuinely new can be threatening because it does not fit into a category to which people have become comfortable and accustomed. The natural tendency of an authority figure, even someone seeking to help the group, is to try to control the process and not accept chaos, messiness, or error. But in the context of creative work the process is inherently uncontrollable, very messy, and filled with error.

In managing the space, you do not want to take up the space. Often formal or informal authority figures take up the space when they use their dominance to assert their point of view, or when the group in their anxiety and frustration look to authority to guide them out of the ambiguity of their adventure. You must resist expressing dominance and resist succumbing to the seductive pleas of people to save them when they are wallowing in uncertainty, even despair. Dominance or dependence on authority may lead to the imposition of, or attachment to, a false and easy solution that has little boundary-transcending capacity.

You must also manage the group boundary to keep the boundary keepers from snuffing out the fires of creativity. The psychologist Rollo May wrote that creativity provokes the jealousy of the gods.[34] He was right. You should be prepared to encounter opposition from powerful people who see themselves as the boundary keepers of the group and do not value creativity, experimentation, or exploration on behalf of transcending boundaries. As discussed in previous chapters, boundary keepers are protectors of the prevailing order and group narratives. They are inclined to seek to honor and protect what a group has done in the past rather than support the boundary-transcending work that must be done to move the group into the future. They make dogmatic declarations about group boundaries and what should and should not be done. The function of dogma, however, is to limit possibilities and limit creativity in the group. Their expressions of dogma are an appeal to cease from exploration and go home. They see play and exploratory work as threatening, frivolous, and a waste of time and resources.

Boundary keepers are generally good people who believe that protecting the boundary and keeping people from transcending the boundary is the right thing to do. Boundary-transcending work is an adventure—and as with any adventure, you might get lost and never return. So naturally the boundary keepers will be a voice of warning and caution, even an outright impediment. The dynamic, between the change agent and the boundary keepers can generate tension within a group—people want to experiment and explore, but they also do not want to be the recipients of the "wrath of the gods." Boundary-transcending work therefore generates tremendous cognitive dissonance that must be managed.

In dealing with obstreperous boundary keepers, explain to them what you feel needs to be done. Keep them informed in order to minimize the threat. It is also important to honor them and not be disrespectful of their thoughts or role. To seriously listen to them and consider their points of view can help enroll them as a supporter and may even lead to their participation in the creative work or at least their assistance in protecting the creative space.

Sometimes, however, even your best intentions may not sway boundary keepers to respect the creative space necessary for boundary-transcending change. Especially on an extremely critical adaptive challenge, where the stakes are high and considerable creativity and exploration are needed, the change agent must be prepared to make difficult choices: do we retreat to the confines of the boundary, or do we risk disappointing the boundary keepers and pursue the adventure anyway?

If boundary-transcending work must be pursued, then risks must be taken. Under such conditions, you must tap great courage and a compelling sense of purpose. The next chapter describes how you can expand your own personal boundaries of self-development, deepening your capacity to lead change courageously in complex, uncertain environments.

TRANSCENDING BOUNDARIES
QUESTIONS FOR PRACTICE

1. What is the purpose of the adventure? What is at stake that necessitates the transcending of boundaries?

2. How can you prepare people for the adventure of moving into unchartered territory? What are the opportunities, and what are the dangers?

3. Do people understand the role of failure in generating a discovery or breakthrough?

4. How can you harness and manage the power of diversity for creative gains? What diverse perspectives and voices need to be included?

5. Are you prepared to manage conflicts and collisions in order to take creative exploration to a higher level?

6. How can you orchestrate informal surprise encounters to spark novel and unconsidered perspectives?

7. How can you promote play? What might it look like? What dogma and boundary markers must you watch for that might stifle play and the creative process?

8. What experiments do you need to conduct? What might be the indicators of progress?

9. How can you hold the creative space and keep the boundary keepers from stopping the adventure or smothering creative sparks?

CHAPTER 6

Building Bridges

Connecting Groups Divided by Deep Fractures

W hen deep, wide fractures develop between groups and people refuse to work together to address shared challenges, the leadership task is to help groups build a bridge of connection and understanding. The work necessitates helping groups modify their perceptions of the other, to transcend their tribalizing impulses, and to work together on behalf of creating a shared future. Specifically, bridge building over fractures is needed when

- unresolved issues in the present or from the past are causing friction and enmity;
- competing priorities have led to misunderstandings, growing tension, or outright conflict; or
- groups are simply a mystery to one another, and the mystery generates suspicion and divisions.

This critical leadership work must be pursued with sensitivity, patience, and wisdom. Even professionals in this field struggle, as the former secretary general of the United Nations, Boutros Boutros-Ghali, can attest.

In his role as head of the UN, Boutros-Ghali met with representatives from each faction of the Hutus and Tutsis in a Rwandan hotel in 1995. The previous year, the Hutus had slaughtered nearly a million people in one hundred days. Tit-for-tat revenge killings and communal strife continued long after. Enraged, the two sides were ready to start another war. Michael Ignatieff, a journalist at the time who was traveling with the secretary general, recorded what happened in that meeting:

> I am invited to sit in on the process of preventive diplomacy at work. Boutros-Ghali is at the head of a baize table in his hotel and listens to the Hutu and Tutsi leadership, ranged on opposite sides, facing each other. The Hutus insist that the Tutsi-dominated Army is waging a campaign of extermination; the Tutsis say that night attacks by Hutu extremists have rendered all constitutional dialogue impossible. The atmosphere in the room thickens with the accusation, counter-accusations, stares, and contempt.
>
> Boutros-Ghali says nothing until everyone has finished speaking. He then tells them they make him ashamed to call himself an African. You seem to assume, he says, that the international community will save you. The international community is quite content to let you massacre each other to the last man. The donor community is fatigued. It is tired of having to save societies that seem incapable of saving themselves. He brings the flat of his palm down upon the baize table. "You are mature adults," he says. "God helps those who help themselves. Your enemy is not each other but fear and cowardice. You must have

enough courage to accept compromises. You must assume your responsibilities. If you don't, nobody will save you." He then sweeps up his papers and strides out.[1]

One can understand the secretary general's frustration and appreciate the way it was expressed. Exasperated, Boutros-Ghali was tired of the unwillingness of the parties to compromise and work harder in taking the first steps to get beyond their enmity. Although a powerful authority figure, charged with the responsibility of attending to these demanding problems, the best he could do was rebuke them. Bridge-building work is complex because an array of emotions, combined with competing interpretations of who is at fault, makes it difficult to see clearly what needs to be done to take positive steps forward.

In determining the kinds of problems for which bridge-building leadership is needed, you might think of a continuum. At one end are extreme conflicts, like that faced by Boutros-Ghali in Rwanda, and at the other end is the tension or misunderstandings of groups that are simply a mystery to one another. Along that continuum will be an array of conflicts, fractures, and fault lines that demand leadership. For example, the work is needed not only in the midst of conflict, like that between the Hutus and Tutsis, but also as a preventive measure, before conflict. When groups are drifting apart and refusing to talk with the other, bridge building must begin. Bridge-building work is also necessary after a conflict to help groups let go of their pain and bitterness, heal, and move on. If people cannot let go, the pain becomes a burden to carry and the conflict might reemerge or get passed to the next generation.

Bridge-building work is not just about addressing intense conflicts between communities, tribes, or nations; it is also important for corporations and institutions that must create intergroup or even global networks and project teams that can get beyond their cultural differences around control of resources, status, sharing of information, and communication approaches to create something of value. If groups experience quarrels, deep resentments, or disdain, their productivity and performance will suffer, and therefore bridge-building work is needed.

Identify Competing Narratives and Sacred Values

The first challenge in bridge building is to appreciate the competing group narratives pertaining to the fracture. How do group narratives and groups' sacred values perpetuate the problem, and what values and perspectives can be leveraged for the promotion of a better relationship?

The groups on each side of the divide might know one another, but in a negative way. Often when in conflict, groups are inclined to scapegoat other groups and assign all blame and responsibility to them. They might even dehumanize the other group by describing them as soulless, immoral, ugly, or useless. The leadership task is to clarify the big assumption each group has about the other and get to the specifics of what happened that produced the fracture. When hearing tales of blame and scapegoating, inquire further to find the actual hard data that led to the formulation of the big assumption. You might ask, "What is it that they specifically did that led you to feel offended, angry, or frustrated?" Or, "When you say they cannot be trusted, what has led you to that conclusion?" The aim is to "unconceal" the groups' cultural narratives as they pertain to people's competing interpretations about how the fracture began and why it persists.

Your challenge is also to gain insight into the sacred values of each group, because to make progress in bridge building, these sacred values might need to be adjusted or reinterpreted.[2] Sacred values inform a group's sense of right or wrong and are a factor in determining what is worth fighting for and even dying for. The group considers these values essential for their identity and survival. They become a rallying call to mobilize people to defend the sacred against the profane. "Give me liberty or give me death" is an example from U.S. history. Additional examples of sacred values include religious ideals, the family name, land or territory, honoring the ancestors, masculine identity, democracy, the free market, and the right to self-expression. These are all abstract concepts, but individuals and groups assign specific meaning and interpretations to their sacred values according to contextual dynamics. For example, the conflict over gun control in the United States is expressed and reinforced by each side appealing to sacred values, particularly after random acts of gun violence when emotions are high and people demand action. One side uses the Founding Fathers and the Constitution as rationale for the right to bear arms, while another side talks about human life and community well-being to support stricter gun laws. Both sides appeal to sacred values as justification for their stance.[3]

You must try to understand what the sacred values are for each group, how the sacred values contribute to the fractured relationship, and what each group is willing to do to protect or promote their values at the expense of doing bridge-building adaptive work. This will help you to appreciate how deep the divides are between groups and how far each group needs to travel in the bridge-building process.

Reduce the Mystery of the Other

A significant reason for a gulf between groups is that groups are often a mystery to one another. That mystery, in turn, can generate suspicion and distrust. In building bridges, the challenge is to reduce the mystery and to help groups not only understand the other but to see them as a valuable resource and potential partner.

Deploy Frontier Guides

Reducing the mystery takes time, but the process can be facilitated by what I call frontier guides—people of credibility and respect who are willing to do three things: (1) go to the boundary frontiers and even venture into "foreign territory" to meet with the other to discover shared values; (2) be a voice of calm and encouragement to their own faction to explore the possibility of a relationship with the other group; and (3) play a mediating role by serving as an "interpreter" of the other group's behavior, sacred values, and aspirations to their own group, and vice versa, in order to start building a relationship. What follows is an example from American diplomacy that illustrates all three functions of frontier guides.

In 1971, China and the United States generated an informal relationship that led to more formal bridge-building work through Ping-Pong.[4] *Time* magazine called it "The ping heard round the world." Nine players and four officials stepped across a bridge from Hong Kong to the Chinese mainland and became the first group of Americans allowed into China since the Communist takeover in 1949. Premier Chou En-lai told the visiting Americans, "You have opened a new chapter in the relations of the American and Chinese people." Three months later, the U.S. Secretary of State, Henry Kissinger, made a secret visit to Peking, and in February 1972, President Richard Nixon made a formal visit, thereby starting the normalization of diplomatic relationships.[5]

A frontier guide—as a formal authority figure like Nixon or as an ordinary person like a Ping-Pong player—can explain to their group why building the bridge is necessary, why the fracture must be transcended, and what common values might connect the groups. They must speak to the cultural narrative of their own people as it pertains to the narrative of yesterday, acknowledging what happened in the past and why change is necessary; to the narrative of us, explaining why a new relationship must be pursued and boundaries expanded; and to the narrative of tomorrow, describing where they hope the bridge will lead as the two groups move into the future.

Richard Nixon played this role for the American people in 1972. Many people were deeply suspicious of China and thought his visit was wrong—after all, the two countries had been enemies since 1949. When Nixon returned from Peking, he spoke to the American people and explained:

> In the last 30 years, Americans have in three different wars gone off by the hundreds of thousands to fight, and some to die, in Asia and in the Pacific. One of the central motives behind my journey to China was to prevent that from happening a fourth time to another generation of Americans. As I have often said, peace means more than the mere absence of war. . . . A gulf of almost 12,000 miles and 22 years of non-communication and hostility separated the United States from the 750 million people who live in the People's Republic of China, and that is one-fourth of all the people in the world. As a result of this trip, we have started the long process of building a bridge across that gulf. . . . We have demonstrated that nations with very deep and fundamental differences can learn to discuss those differences calmly, rationally, and frankly.[6]

The frontier guide can also serve as a "cultural interpreter" by explaining to their group what they observed, what the other group is like, and what they share in common, thereby reducing the mystery of the other in a way that makes sense to their people. If they can go further and explain what the groups have in common and what is unique about the other group in a way that piques interest, they can lower defenses and evoke positive emotions that encourage others to engage in bridge building.

In promoting adaptive work, small acts, such as a game of Ping-Pong, can make a big difference. The challenge is to find an activity, sacred value, or enjoyable practice that is shared, and begin from there. This phenomenon is what the psychologist Gordon Allport called "contact theory," which essentially argues that the more people can interact informally with members of another group, the greater the opportunity for decreasing misunderstandings and increasing appreciation for the other.[7] In one major study in Europe, more than 3,800 people were asked about their attitudes toward minority groups and whether they had any friends of another nationality, race, culture, religion, or social class. On a psychological test, those people with minority friends reported higher scores for sympathy and admiration for others who are different from themselves and lower scores for prejudice on a psychological test.[8]

Informal contact is an emotional exercise. Anxiety usually accompanies the initial encounters between groups, but as people come to know one another, that anxiety decreases. Of course, if a person has a negative encounter, the anxiety can increase. The leadership work is to monitor the reactions of groups and intervene to help people make sense of what is happening, to calm people when offended, and to encourage people along in their bridge-building efforts.

Orchestrate Bridging Conversations

When enough of an informal relationship is established, the leadership work is to orchestrate bridging conversations. Bridging conversations prompt groups to "go toward the fire." Going toward the fire is a metaphor for seeking the burning reasons that people are suspicious of the other, have disdain for them, or are refusing to collaborate. Your role in helping groups go toward the fire is to be the conversation manager—to prod people, ask tough questions, and help the groups persist, even when the topics get hot. Leadership work entails getting groups to speak and examine their sacred values, big assumptions, and competing perspectives and also their hurt, pain, or disappointment—even though such emotions might be difficult to express and difficult for others to hear.

Tough conversations can get heated, and therefore you will need to regulate the levels of heat each group can tolerate pertaining to the intensity of engagement. You must also manage the mood, promote clarity, and look for commonality and openings for connection. The mood needs to encourage the expression of competing perspectives. The conversation should not be dominated by any one individual or faction but should be conducive for everyone to express their point of view. You might need to slow the conversation down to ensure that one point is dealt with at a time. You might need to play the cultural interpreter role, helping one group to understand what the other group is really saying. You might also invite each of the respective groups to respond and offer counterperspectives, different interpretations, confirmation, or additional information. Ultimately, the challenge is to help each group understand the other—to work through the abstract and competing interpretations and discover the one thing everyone cares about that serves to generate a foundation for promoting and encouraging bridge-building work.

Discuss the Undiscussable

In going toward the fire, a key principle is to help groups "discuss the undiscussable" and engage in straight talk.[9] Discussing the undiscussable means helping people say what they need to say but what they fear to say. It is about being explicit in describing how they feel, why they feel the way they do, and what they think about the other. People are generally afraid of having deep conversations because they sense the discussion is going to be emotionally draining, someone's feelings might get hurt, or the conversation will blaze out of control. All these things can be true occasionally, as we have all experienced, but there are also times when issues get clarified, problems get resolved, wounds are healed, agreements are made, and change unfolds.

Bridge-building conversations require courage on the part of both the change agent and the divided groups, particularly when conversations get heated. Many people's natural instinct then is to flee, and the instinct of some is to fight. Anticipating these reactions and knowing how to deal with them is a critical leadership skill.

I once joined the president of Madagascar in a closed-door meeting in Zambia with the presidents of a number of southern African countries to have a confidential conversation with President Robert Mugabe of Zimbabwe about the upcoming presidential election in his country. Zimbabwe at that time was teetering on collapse, with inflation running at more than 1,000 percent. It looked like the election would be far from democratic, as opposition politicians were being beaten and jailed. The chairman of the meeting was the president of Zambia, Levy Mwanawasa, a gentle and benevolent man. The meeting began with Mwanawasa expressing his concern for the electoral process in Zimbabwe and his desire to have a forthright conversation about the upcoming election and troubles that were going on. Mugabe immediately interrupted the chairman and accused him of being a puppet of the Western powers. There was an awkward silence in the room, and everyone looked to the chairman to see what he would do. President Mwanawasa took a deep breath and said, "Okay, let's go to lunch." The meeting ended and the tough conversation about Zimbabwe's election never took place—and, as a postscript, Zimbabwe's election was a disaster.

While President Mwanawasa displayed courage to raise a tough issue, he succumbed to Mugabe's ploy. He also needed to be supported by other leaders in the room, but such support was not forthcoming. In fact, one leader even sided with Mugabe! This example underscores the unpredictable complexity of tough bridge-building conversations, as well as the necessity for a conversation manager to keep a cool head when the discussion grows heated or people try to flee from responsibility for the problem.

Discussing the undiscussable requires surfacing and discussing people's deep concerns, what they really think and feel, and the assumptions underlying their logic. People generally express their concerns or evaluations in abstract terms.

To make progress, the change agent acting as conversation manager helps groups go from abstract generalizations about each other and the problem to the specifics of what happened that led to the formation of their respective interpretations of the problem, the accompanying emotional sentiments, and the actions they have taken to perpetuate the fracture. The leadership task is to help people (1) see how their interpretation of the problem emerged and could be the product of a flawed assumption, or (2) clarify the sacred value underlying people's actions—a value that the people themselves do not fully appreciate as it pertains to why they react the way they do.

This process is called "descending the ladder of interpretation."[10] Descending the ladder of interpretation is about taking an abstract generalization and seeking to ground it and make it as objective as you can by getting people to explain, illustrate, and explore their interpretations. This is a process of inquiry and clarification that requires considerable skill to do well. If you are to provide leadership to build bridges, you must help people move from their abstract interpretations about the other to the specifics in order to begin a process of reinterpretation.

Imagine a ladder with many rungs. The highest rung is a generalization about the other group such as "They are bad people." At the bottom of the ladder is the concrete, specific data of what actually happened. As the conversation manager, you need to bring people down the ladder of interpretation. When a group says the other group is bad, you might ask, "Why are they bad?" The response could be "Because they cannot be trusted." You must bring them down another rung on the ladder by asking, "Why can't they be trusted?" They might say, "Because they didn't support us in the technology integration project." You must now bring them down yet another rung. "When you say they didn't support you, what specifically did they do?" "Well, they didn't show up at the meetings and they sabotaged the process." "How many meetings did they miss, and how did they sabotage the process?" "They missed two meetings, and they sabotaged us because we did not get sufficient funding, and I think they are responsible." "Did you ask them why they missed the meetings, and how do you know they are specifically responsible for the lack of funding?"

You must help the group descend the ladder of interpretation to clarify the sacred value that is informing their actions. For example, the award-winning documentary *Black Harvest* presents the problem of a businessman in the traditional highlands of Papua New Guinea and his attempts to establish a coffee plantation.[11] Even though the community agreed to the business venture, most of the men refused to do the work of picking coffee beans. The exasperated entrepreneur, Joe Leahy, repeatedly rebuked the men, but to no avail. Rather than pick coffee beans, they preferred to go to war against their neighbors. As a result, the coffee plantation collapsed.

The leadership task when a group is in conflict is to find out the sacred value that has a grasp on people. Employing the ladder of interpretation, you can descend the rungs of the ladder in stages that look something like this:

Man: We cannot pick coffee today, because we must go and fight.

Change agent: Why must you fight?

Man: It is really the fight of the other tribe, but we are obligated to help. It doesn't matter the reason for the fight—we have to help our friends.

Change agent: But the enemies of your friends are not your enemies, and now you are making new enemies and your own men are dying. Besides, you made a commitment to pick coffee and make this plantation succeed so your people can benefit.

Man: Yes, but we are men and fearless warriors, and it will not be honorable if we do not stand up for our friends.

Change agent: And now you are making new enemies, your own men are dying, and your plantation is falling apart. Are you sure you want to make all these sacrifices to keep on fighting? You cannot make progress in building a business unless you deal with the sacred values of manhood, fighting, and obligations to your allies. Are you willing to do that?

Going down the ladder of interpretation eventually leads to the sacred values of the group. In this context, two sacred values emerged that are more important than helping a coffee plantation be successful: (1) the obligations and loyalties to one's clansmen and allies, and (2) the ritualistic activities of fighting and proving one's manhood.

When people can see their sacred values in front of them, the adaptive work can begin. They can appreciate how those values generate fractures, conflict, and loss, and lead them to pursue one set of commitments over another. It may help them rethink and even readjust aspects of their sacred values on behalf of generating bridge-building progress. If people are unaware of what really is holding them back, they will find it difficult to let go, move forward, or reinterpret their sacred values in a way that brings them closer to the other.

Keep People in the Room

When a deep fracture exists between groups, tough conversations on behalf of bridge building invariably generate a lot of heat—the heat of disagreement, misunderstanding, and contention. The natural instinct is fight or flight. As the conversation manager, to keep people talking, you must remind them of the higher purpose—what benefits are possible if a bridge can be built, and what losses might ensue if not. You also need to be sensitive to what is pulling them out of the room. Often people worry they are being disloyal to their faction or violating a sacred value if they try to build a relationship with the other. They personally might want to build that bridge, but their factional obligations generate hesitancy.

Former U.S. president Jimmy Carter is known for his extraordinary bridge-building work in bringing Israel and Egypt together to sign the Camp David peace agreement in 1978. Both President

Anwar Sadat of Egypt and Prime Minister Menachem Begin of Israel threatened to leave the thirteen-day negotiation multiple times, and Carter was continuously trying to keep them engaged in the process and not let their differences become too much of an impediment. Both men were under enormous pressure from their respective factions to not sign an agreement, which made the challenge almost impossible. At one point Begin had had enough and was getting ready to leave. Carter gave Begin an autographed photo of the three of them (Begin, Sadat, and Carter) as a gift for each of his eight grandchildren. Carter recalled:

> He was hardly speaking to me. . . . I handed him the photographs. He said, "Thank you, Mr. President" and turned around, dismissing me in effect. As he looked at the photographs, . . . one by one he read out the names of his grandchildren. Tears ran down his cheeks, and when I saw them I also cried. And he said, "Why don't we try one more time?"[12]

Another time, Sadat called for his helicopter and wanted to leave. "I was distressed because Sadat had promised me he would not leave," Carter recalled.

> I went over to the window, and I looked out over the mountain side and said a silent prayer. Then I went and confronted Sadat. It was the only harsh confrontation we ever had. I told him that he had betrayed me and broken his promise to me—that if he left Camp David and left me and the Israelis there, the condemnation of the world would be on him. And eventually he decided to stay.[13]

Had Jimmy Carter not played that bridge-building role, the historic accord would never have been signed. The challenge of the change agent is to keep people in the room. They must be reminded of the higher purpose and be encouraged to transcend their group boundaries and tribal loyalties, for the moment at least, to find common ground.

Promote Perspective Taking to "Reinterpret" the Other

Ultimately, the challenge in bridge building is to help each group see something of themselves in the other. This can be enhanced through perspective taking. A group might not agree with the other, but the challenge is to help the group understand where they are coming from. If a group feels harmed or hurt, the natural inclination is for people to delegitimize or desensitize themselves to the perspectives, concerns, and suffering of their opponents. But when groups come together and can tell their story with the spirit of listening and learning, insights and even empathy can emerge. For example, one study found that a positive change in attitude occurred for Israelis and Palestinians after they engaged in exercises that encouraged perspective taking.[14]

You can promote perspective taking by getting groups to explain how they would feel if they were in the same situation and experienced a similar event. What emotions would they experience? Given their emotions, how might they react? Emotional perspective taking can lead groups to see the humanity of the other and find a common connection.[15]

Perspective taking also includes learning about and acknowledging the sacred values and cultural narratives of others. Too often a group will consider its own values as sacred but fail to appreciate the values of others as important and sacred to them. When a group is given an opportunity to express their sacred values and narratives, and they feel they are heard and listened to respectfully, the relationship between two opposing groups is enhanced.[16] Understandably, it is not easy for a group to acknowledge the sacred values of another, particularly when the values are substantially different. But values are often abstractions that can be interpreted loosely or literally.[17] The challenge is to generate some human connection, even if it is small and tenuous, by finding something in each group's sacred values and narratives that can serve as a bond that keeps people engaged, as painful and difficult as it might be.

Sometimes, given the intensity of the conflict, the politics involved, and feelings of betrayal of their faction should they participate, people might be unwilling to engage in perspective taking. The timing might not be right. But eventually, perhaps after the heat of conflict has waned, bridge-building perspective taking might be needed to heal old wounds and make sense of what happened in order to extract lessons and clean up any mess remaining.

Twenty-three years after the Vietnam War ended, Robert McNamara, the former U.S. secretary of defense, conducted bridge-building conversations with his Vietnamese counterparts in 1997. With a degree of suspicion and hesitation, the two sides met in Hanoi for four days to extract lessons from the war. Why did it happen? What were the big assumptions each side had about the other? What were the missed opportunities to bring the war to an early end? McNamara was eighty-one years old at the time, yet in the spirit of learning, friendship, and even contrition, he initiated the meeting to ensure that such a war would never happen again.[18] It was a trying and exasperating experience, and McNamara confessed that at one time they "almost came to blows," but the experience was extraordinary.[19] He learned about the narrative of nationalism that drove the Vietnamese to fight first the French and then the Americans. He also learned that each side had very different and flawed interpretations of the other's motives. After these conversations, McNamara concluded that the Vietnam War was a mistake: "We were wrong, terribly wrong," he said, "and we owe it to future generations to explain why."[20] His biggest regret was that he and his fellow American policy makers did not do the critical perspective-taking work decades earlier. If they had, the war might never have happened. At the time, they were locked into a set of big assumptions that were flawed, and neither side really appreciated or understood the narratives and sacred values of the other. The Americans believed they were fighting a war against communism, while the Vietnamese had nationalistic goals and pursued the war to protect themselves from imperialism.

What Robert McNamara did was a courageous act of bridge-building leadership. Too often after a conflict, groups walk away and fail to do the adaptive work of learning from the conflict: understanding why it happened, how each group contributed to the conflict, and what opportunities were missed that might have brought the conflict to earlier resolution. When groups fail to do that work, the enmity or fault lines persist and may be woven negatively into group cultural narratives, making bridge building difficult for subsequent generations.

Help People to Cross the Bridge

Once the bridge is built, the adaptive work is for people to step onto the bridge and cross it. People need to find sufficient courage to move toward the other and let go of whatever it is that is holding them back, and to see that an inclusive future has greater promise than a divided past or an exclusive future.

Speak the Narrative of We

To promote the crossing of the bridge, you need to speak publicly and powerfully the new *narrative of we*. Suspicion and distrust will persist unless you, other change agents, and key boundary keepers speak the new narrative in a way that gets people's attention and helps them to adjust to a more inclusive possibility.

Abraham Lincoln at Gettysburg intervened to shift the narrative of the country to make it more inclusive during a period of bitter rivalry. He went to Gettysburg, Pennsylvania, in 1863 to dedicate the national cemetery where nearly fifty thousand men had died on the battlefield five months earlier. He gave a short speech letting people know that it was time to start the bridge-building work of uniting a fractured nation. Lincoln sought to reframe the narrative of two competing groups—the North and the South—as a narrative of we. He reminded people of the American Revolution and Declaration of Independence, two critical stories both sides shared in common pertaining to their narrative of yesterday.

The timing of the speech was perfect as it captured the attention and imagination of a weary nation. In delivering the speech, Lincoln embodied that weariness, while also embodying the hope. His assistant noted that when he delivered the speech, his face had "a ghastly color" and that he was "sad, mournful, almost haggard."[21] In fact, Lincoln was feverish with smallpox and totally exhausted, yet he clearly knew what was at stake. He was able to reach deep within his reservoir of wisdom and let people know—on both sides—that they could not wallow in resentment and hatred for each other but had to rebuild the nation by embracing a higher and uniting aspiration.[22]

A new aspiration must be sufficient to extricate people from their silos, thwart the tribal impulse, help people sustain painful losses, and get them working together for a common purpose. Bridge building is a process of expanding boundaries. It is about reducing the threat of the other, changing the interpretation, and relating to the other as a potential partner and ally. Depending on the nature of the fracture, refashioning the narrative will take time, because a degree of suspicion and mystery might linger.[23] Socially learned stereotypes and historical events add to the resilience of an exclusive narrative. Modifying the narrative is therefore a process that must be paced, not forced. Moving too fast might provide the illusion of inclusivity, but the bonds lack the strength to sustain the relationship.

To move great numbers of people to embrace the narrative of we and to cross the bridge, you might use symbols that resonate with the hesitant faction. Nelson Mandela did just that. He had been president for less than a year when he used the 1995 Rugby World Cup final to make a bridge-building intervention between black and white South Africans. Just before the game began, Mandela walked out onto the center of the field to shake hands with the national team and wish them well. He was wearing the green jersey of the Springboks, who were a predominantly white team and loathed by black South Africans because they represented the former racist system of apartheid. On the back of Mandela's jersey was the number 6, the number of the team's captain, François Pienaar. Sixty-five thousand people were in the stadium, nearly all of them white; clearly moved by Mandela's gesture, they collectively shouted, "Nelson! Nelson! Nelson!" Pienaar had grown up considering Mandela a terrorist. He said he was so overwhelmed by the experience that he had to bite his lip to keep himself from crying.[24] The event was a turning point for Pienaar and for the rest of the country, and he personally became close friends with Mandela and later asked him to be the godfather to his children

Timing is critical in making symbolic interventions. Of course, not everyone has the stature of Nelson Mandela, but within any group are respected formal and informal authority figures who can step forward and speak a new narrative of we, literally with their words or symbolically through their actions.

Help People to Let Go of the Past

Sometimes the mess of the past remains in the present. Something is lingering in the hearts and minds of people, in their group cultural narrative, that leads to hesitation in crossing the bridge. The leadership task is to find out what is holding people back, help them to let go, and encourage them forward.

Letting go is a release from the prison of the past, be it anger, disappointment, or contempt, in order to get on with one's life in the present and to move unshackled into the future. It is a process of transition. Transitions can be aided by symbolic gestures, rituals, ceremonies, and shared group activities.

If there has been great suffering and loss, letting go and transitioning may require genuine mourning. If people cannot mourn, the danger is that the conflict will be carried into the future, as people feel obligated to defend their fallen comrades, family members, ancestors, or tribal friends.[25] Mourning is a process of lament that can create the space to transition into the future.

Sometimes in healing wounds and getting people onto the bridge, symbolic but heartfelt gestures need to be made to acknowledge the mistakes of the past and to ask for forgiveness. An apology can be a powerful expression of regret and serve to clean up the mess and reduce the potency of the sentiments that make people hesitant to cross the bridge.[26] For example, in February 2008, the Australian prime minister Kevin Rudd apologized to the Aboriginal people for the behavior and policies of the government decades earlier as it pertained to the "stolen generation." He said that these policies "inflicted profound grief, suffering, and loss" as thousands of Aboriginal children were taken from their parents and extended families and placed in orphanages or adopted out to white families. "For the indignity and degradation thus inflicted on a proud people and a proud culture," said the prime minister, "we say sorry."[27] In the context of Australia, to have the head of the nation publicly declare that serious mistakes had been made in the past that caused great suffering that persisted in the present was an important step in the work of reconciliation, healing, and the creation of a new narrative of we.

Sometimes to get people to cross the bridge, some form of recompense is required. It might be necessary to get the group that caused offense to make amends to the group that has been hurt, harmed, or suffered loss. Recompense might require compensation, community work, or some form of sacrifice and investment in time and resources that sends a message that one is genuinely regretful and committed to moving forward together. There is a growing movement around the world on restorative justice that addresses this aspect of bridge building.[28] Restorative justice is people centered rather than legally centered. In providing leadership, you might ask, "What is it that people want from the offending group, or need to see and hear from the other, that can encourage people to cross the bridge?"

Sometimes, to move people to cross the bridge, what might be required is the expression of forgiveness. In the opening foreword of this book, the Dalai Lama says that in an interdependent world, compassion and warm-heartedness are required. The ultimate expression of compassion and warm-heartedness is forgiveness. You should deliberate deeply with others to determine whether the expression of forgiveness is the appropriate intervention to advance the work—for the group offering it and the group receiving it. Forgiving others does not mean letting people "off the hook," but creating the space for a relationship that transcends the offense and as a way to heal a broken group.

I began this chapter by talking about how an exasperated UN secretary general struggled to provide bridge-building leadership in Rwanda at the end of the genocide. Since that horrific event, some of the most inspiring bridge-building leadership has been provided not by diplomats or politicians, but by ordinary people such as the Rwandan singer Jean-Paul Samputu.

Samputu was performing in Europe at the time of the genocide in 1994, but he soon found out that his entire family had been killed, and one of the murderers was his childhood friend and neighbor, Vincent. Because Samputu was an international performer, he had charged his best friend with the task of taking care of his family while he was away. The shock of the loss of his family and the knowledge that his friend was a culprit was too much for him to bear. Over the next decade, Samputu suffered from depression and drug abuse. "I lost my mind," he said. "Every day I drank to forget. It was like I was in hell. I wanted to kill Vincent, and since I couldn't kill him, I started to kill myself."

In 2007, Samputu did what he felt he had to do to move on with his life: he decided to meet personally with Vincent and to tell him that he forgave him. "Telling him this gave me a great peace in my heart," he said. "I was a healed man. Afterwards we went to share a meal together." Their friendship was reborn, and they spent the next few years speaking as a team to other Rwandans on reconciliation and healing.[29]

Although few people can do what Jean Paul Samputu did, from a leadership point of view, you must gauge the situation and readiness of both groups for such an intimate and emotional process.

Helping groups cross the bridge and ensuring that the narrative of we has resilience and sustainability is a process that needs imagination, time, and attention. In spite of your best leadership efforts, there may be some people who refuse to make the transition. Some might find it too painful; their narrative of victimization or resentment has such a grasp on them that they cannot let go. These people need additional time and support, and even then they might never cross. Some people might be so hurt, angry, and loyal to the old narrative that they not only refuse to cross the bridge but they seek to stop others from crossing. Some might even try to blow up the bridge. The situation must be monitored to see who is embracing the transition, who is hesitating, and who might sabotage the process. Being cognizant of where people are emotionally, and tapping your strong network of boundary keepers and fellow change agents who can support the reluctant ones, will help minimize risks.

After the Bridge Is Built, Keep Tribalizing Impulses from Undermining Gains

Even after the bridge has been built, leadership is needed to keep the tribalizing impulse from rearing and undermining all the important work that groups have done to build and cross the bridge. Some people might refuse to let go of fracturing behaviors because they see these behaviors as an expression of their group cultural narrative and, to them, honoring their group cultural narrative is more important than sustaining a relationship with the other group. They might intentionally or unintentionally subvert the relationship that has been established by acting in ways that might be considered insensitive and disrespectful by others.

For example, a group in Virginia in the United States repeatedly flies the Confederate flag, a flag that represents the days of slavery for many Americans.[30] The group, the Virginia Flaggers, says they want to commemorate their ancestors who fought and died for the South in the Civil War. In June 2014, in a very visible public area, they flew a flag standing 80 feet high and measuring 20 by 30 feet, thereby offending many people.[31] When groups tribalize and advance their narratives in fracturing ways, fault lines might be activated.

In 2013, the navy of Indonesia also did some tribalizing to advance their cultural and political narrative in a way that was unintentionally fracturing and disrespectful to their neighbor, Singapore. They named a frigate to honor two soldiers who, in 1965, ignited a bomb in Singapore's downtown area, killing three people and wounding more than thirty.[32] The two men were captured and hanged by the Singapore authorities. The bombing was in the context of President Sukarno's confrontation with his regional neighbors to thwart what he saw as neocolonial expansionism. While Indonesia has gone through dramatic changes since that period and is a growing economic powerhouse and democracy with 250 million people, some Indonesians still regard the two bombers as heroes. The Indonesian foreign minister explained that they meant no ill by naming the ship after the soldiers, but the reality was that for Singaporeans, this act opened an old wound.[33]

Insensitive tribalizing impulses, whether they are symbols, policies, or fracturing comments that are publicly expressed, by design or in the heat of the moment, that generate tensions or a wobble on the bridge, need to be dealt with swiftly. If they are left to linger, the tension might lead people to retreat back to their side of the bridge, and the great gains will be lost, or fault lines might be activated. Therefore, the leadership challenge is to contain divisive tribalizing behavior and the advancement of a group's narrative when it is insensitive, disrespectful, or potentially offensive to others. This work might necessitate going to your own people, or to the other group, to put a spotlight on fracturing acts and tendencies, explaining why maintaining the bridge is vital work and how insensitivities can undermine the investment in time, sacrifice, and resources that groups on both sides have already made.

As a final note, it is important for groups to acknowledge and celebrate the efforts that have generated a healthy relationship. Like any relationship, moments of tension and insult will surface from time to time. The key lies in not taking the relationship for granted but ensuring that enough people on both sides do the maintenance work of sustaining the bridge.

BUILDING BRIDGES
QUESTIONS FOR PRACTICE

1. What is the nature of the fracture that requires building a bridge?

2. How do group narratives reinforce the great divide?

3. If groups are a mystery to one another, how might you provide leadership to reduce the mystery?

4. Who can serve as frontier guides?

5. As a bridging conversation manager, how can you help groups go toward the fire and examine the essence of the conflict? How can you get people to discuss the undiscussable and do the difficult work of perspective taking?

6. How might you speak and promote the narrative of we? How can you get significant boundary keepers to speak the inclusive narrative? What symbolic acts or gestures might make a difference?

7. How can you help hesitant people find the courage or willingness to cross the bridge?

8. Who might sabotage the bridge-building efforts, and how might you address fracturing acts when they arise?

PART 3

Personal Work

CHAPTER 7

Expanding
Your Personal
Boundaries

To be a global change agent and provide leadership for a fractured world, you must expand your own boundaries of self-understanding and capacity for intervention. Without self-development, you will find it difficult to cross boundaries and operate in complex, uncertain environments, and your behavior might exacerbate the fractures that already exist.

Consider the case of sixty-three-year-old Viktor Yanukovych, the former president of the Ukraine. He was a bright, capable politician with more than twenty-five years of political experience, yet he made some dreadful choices that led to hundreds of people getting killed and him fleeing office in February 2014.[1] He acted in ways that further fragmented his country. Why?

In 2010, when Yanukovych was elected, he faced a major cross-boundary, bridge-building leadership challenge. The country was fractured due to ugly political battles. He had the chance to heal the nation and bring diverse groups together on behalf of a higher purpose, but he did not. He chose hardliners in his own party and placed them in key positions of authority, and the fractures in the nation deepened as a result. He unilaterally decided to renege on the deal for greater integration with the European Union through a free-trade agreement. That was the straw that broke the camel's back—more than half a million people went to the streets insisting that he sign the EU agreement. Chaos resulted, Yanukovych fled, Crimea was annexed by Russia, and in parts of the country civil unrest and fighting ensued.

The Ukraine is a state with diverse political and cultural factions, yet Yanukovych tried to drag the country in a direction that resonated with one faction at the expense of other factions. For many reasons, he wanted to keep the Ukraine in the Russian hemisphere, while other factions wanted greater integration into the European community. He tried to force change, and people rebelled, further fracturing the country.

To provide leadership as a global change agent, you must shift from being a creature of your own faction, as Yanukovych was, to someone who can hold and engage the diverse interests, perspectives, and aspirations of multiple groups. Leadership requires getting other people to expand and cross boundaries, but if you cannot do so yourself, how can you lead?

Expanding your personal boundaries is important to help you become more flexible and multidimensional as a leader, and to be able to adjust your style and approach according to contextual demands. More options become available to you in terms of the role you play and kinds of interventions you can make. At any given time, you might need to play a different role—sage, poet, friend, peacemaker, or warrior, for example—depending on the people you are interacting with and the problem confronting groups. If you are one-dimensional, it is easy to become predictable and parochial, thereby limiting your effectiveness.

Ed Catmull, president of Pixar and Walt Disney Animation Studios, spoke of Steve Jobs's boundary-expanding capacities.

> I do think there are principles for how you think about things, how you explore the boundaries, how you keep yourself from getting caught up in a conservative way of thinking, and a way to keep yourself from being blind to things. Steve had the facility to do that. Most people don't. If a person can work on their personal view of life, and how they tackle problems, and how they open themselves up, they will get a greater result.[2]

Expanding your personal boundaries is about increasing in insight, even wisdom. *Wisdom* is an ancient word that means "the capacity to see." The reality is that as a change agent, one can never see all that is going on because of the complexity of the problem, the complexity of the system, and one's blind spots, personal hungers, and natural predilections to use power in a habitual and predictable way. Although one might not be wise enough to succeed at all times, one should have a passion for wisdom to increase the chances of success. How one goes about the work of change should be a manifestation of that passion. The passion for wisdom should lead to an intense curiosity to see and understand oneself as an instrument of power—"Why do I react the way I do?" "How do I behave under stress?" "How do I deal with complexity?" "How can I use what power I have more effectively, morally, and responsibly?"

To guide you in the process of cultivating enough wisdom and expanding your personal boundaries to exercise leadership, I suggest the following principles. These principles are by no means the definitive statement on how to attain wisdom. I think the sages of the past in all the great cultures and religions of the world have given us some powerful guidelines for the pursuit of wisdom. The principles I offer are insights that come from my interviews with leaders and change agents from around the world, an examination of the latest social science research, and my direct experience observing or participating in many large-scale change initiatives in business, education, government, and international development.

Gain Insight into Your Own Group Cultural Narrative and Personal Biases

Your challenge is to become aware of what values you embody, represent, and even champion so that you can better cross boundaries and navigate the cultural, political, and institutional terrain in which you seek to exercise leadership. You need to know your own sacred values—those values for which you will make sacrifices and perhaps never compromise—and those values that are malleable and flexible. You need to gain insight into your biases and predispositions that lead you act in a particular manner. Given your attachment to particular values and beliefs, you want to have enough wisdom to ensure that you do not become culturally narcissistic, a cultural imperialist, or a tribalizing crusader. That necessitates learning about your own group narrative and how it informs your actions and your approach to leadership and change.

Your group cultural narrative is your personal web of significance (see Chapter 2 on diagnosis). It is one thing to diagnose the group cultural narrative of others, but can you also see how your own narrative shapes and informs your behavior—providing strengths but also constraints? If you cannot, you may be inclined to impose your narrative on others and become "ugly" in their eyes.

Your cultural narrative can also be a tremendous resource, providing a set of values and practices that increase your resilience and help you deal with the turbulence of uncertainty and change. All cultures relate stories of resilience and growth. The symbols embedded in group narratives provide profound psychological comfort. By tapping into those stories, you can find a source of energy that might give you the courage to challenge your own group's maladaptive features and to cross boundaries to work with others.

With insight into your cultural narrative, you also increase your capacity for choice—when to embody your own group's narrative and represent their values, or when to embrace a different group's narrative and champion new values. For example, Gandhi sought to be the embodiment of the noblest virtues and values of Indian tradition while seeking to challenge those aspects of his culture that were maladaptive, such as the caste system and the tribalizing impulses of different groups that damaged society. Even though he was educated as a lawyer in London, he opted to wear a simple loincloth rather than a Western suit because he wanted to engage people as equals by harnessing the symbols of tradition.

Learning about your cultural narrative is like stepping out of your body to look at yourself from a distance to appreciate how powerful cultural currents carry you along and shape your behavior. It necessitates considering fascinating questions such as these:

- **How was your cultural narrative formed?** What was the "story" inculcated in you about who you are, your role in the world, and the role of "your people"? How was that formed? What are "voices" in your head? What are they telling you?

- **What are your aspirations and the key values in your narrative?** Think about your notions of success, progress, and where those notions came from. In other words, what is important to you and why? What might be the limitations of these values and aspirations given the problems we see in the world today?

- **How does your cultural narrative inform your relationship to power and authority, and your view of leadership?** How important is authority to you? What role does it play in your culture? Should authority be challenged? Is authority essential for leadership? Would you like to lead from the center in a position of authority or from the grassroots or the margins? Why?

- **What adaptive challenges do you "resonate" to?** How are the adaptive challenges you want to attend to connected to your cultural narrative and the larger community's cultural narrative? What problems might your narrative lead you to be dismissive of?

- **How is your narrative confining, and how is it empowering?** What are the boundaries to your narrative, and do you feel like you are a prisoner to that narrative? Is the grasp of your community's cultural narrative so powerful that you feel obligated to honor and promote it? Is it possible to transcend it without selling out? Do you feel disloyal when you cross boundaries? How does it give you the strength and the energy to help you in your leadership pursuits as a global change agent?

To learn about your own cultural narrative, you need to reflect deeply on your behavior to ascertain what your sacred values and priorities are and why you do what you do. You also need to encounter other narratives in order to contrast your own. Like a fish in water, it is difficult to see yourself and appreciate your values if you are always in safe, familiar territory. The encounter of difference allows you to interrogate objectively your own values and to see how your cultural narrative shapes the things you care about and your orientation to the world, for better and for ill. In doing so, not only can you gain insight into yourself, your group, and other groups, but you can become more global in mindset and practice—the topic of the next section.

Cultivate a Global Mindset

Crossing boundaries to exercise leadership requires a high level of capability for mental complexity, even a global mindset.[3] A global mindset is about thinking systemically, increasing in cultural understanding, and seeing complexity and nuance.

The opposite of a global mindset is a low-complexity mindset, or a simple, linear way of thinking. The cultural narrative of people with a low-complexity mindset is the source of their truth, and their notion of the truth is unquestionable and not subject to critical examination. They relate to things as black or white, right or wrong, and good or bad. They lack curiosity. Crossing boundaries is threatening and disorienting to them. They value—and will fight to protect—their group boundaries. They can be tribalizing crusaders and they can be good followers, but they are generally ineffective change agents. In a stable world, low-complexity thinking is sufficient to get by; but in a changing interdependent world it presents difficulties.[4]

The person with a global mindset is more tolerant and open to diversity. One's sense of self is not tied exclusively to a particular cultural narrative but is constantly expanding through interaction with different people and groups in unique and challenging contexts. People with a global mindset embrace contradiction and paradox. They are at ease, even tranquil, with complexity. They do not become flustered in times of anxiety but can be still while seeking to interpret what is happening in a way that allows for useful discoveries to be made. Their discoveries are never truths but interpretations that will be subject to further testing and exploration. They are passionately curious and seek to understand the nature of the essence of things, rather than let the inquiry cease at the level of appearance or symptoms. For them, good questions are always more important than answers.

With a global mindset, you will find it easier to transcend self-interest, overcome group loyalties, and build diverse relationships when the challenge calls for it because it allows you to see the complex humanity in all groups. You can appreciate that the world is filled with a rich tapestry of myths, stories, and narratives that enrich the planet and can be harnessed for change. This mindset also enables you to be more multidimensional in leadership style and approach. Familiar with and knowledgeable about diverse groups, you can integrate and employ multiple perspectives and practices from your leadership "toolbox" to spur different groups into action.

Although we live in a globalized world, many people lack a global mindset because they communicate only with like-minded people and communities, be it at work, at home, or through social media. They have no real encounter with differences and avoid experiences that might generate a clash in values, beliefs, or style. Even many expatriates can work for years in another country but never really "experience" the culture. They wine and dine with one another but are strangers to the ordinary people in the host country.

To develop a global mindset, you must find ways to go beyond the confines of your group boundary. That necessitates pursuing multicultural and diversity-related experiences and, when doing so, putting your convictions to the side and being open to novelty, challenge, and surprise. You need to have your own worldview challenged through direct engagement with difference, even if that engagement leads to conflict. Such experiences can be thought-provoking and powerfully enriching, enabling one to better grasp what might be required culturally, politically, and relationally to get important work done.

Recent research also indicates that multicultural and diversity experiences are positively linked to measures of moral judgment, open-mindedness, and creativity.[5] You begin to see people not through the lens of a preconceived stereotype but in a richer and more nuanced way. In fact, such experiences can lead to a significant adjustment, even a transformation, in one's thinking and style.[6] For college students, the research shows that diversity experiences increase the capacity for socially responsible leadership and contribute to intellectual and emotional growth, and critical thinking and problem-solving skills.[7]

As you pursue novel, sundry experiences, you can expect the clash of values, styles, and points of view, but such experiences can result in transformative learning. Your whole notion of what is "normal" might be disrupted. I recently heard an anthropologist say something to the effect that when you initially look at the other, they look a little weird. But as you seek to understand the other, the more normal they become. And then you begin to notice that you are the weird one![8]

Seek Out Boundary-Expanding Partners

You need people around you who can help expand your boundaries rather than reinforce your boundaries. You need people to

partner with you in the creative exploration of ideas and strategy—people that push you, challenge you, and help you grow
multidimensionally as a change agent and as a human being. If
you are going to provide leadership for an interdependent world,
you personally must value the power of interdependence in the
form of partners and collaborators in increasing your leadership
capacity. Indeed, many creative people thrive on interdependence.
It nurtures their work.

In seeking partners, look for people who bring a unity of purpose
and complementarity—that is, they share the greater mission or
higher purpose you are championing. Although their styles and
perspectives might be different, people with a shared purpose can
play off one another to produce something that is distinctive,
even exceptional. The psychologist Lev Vygotsky spoke about
the power that comes from "living in the other's mind" in the
context of productive collaboration. Committed partners develop
a synergistic relationship where they are able to understand what
their partner is thinking, feeling, or trying to accomplish and
where they might be stuck.[9] For example, the English artists
Vanessa Bell (the sister of Virginia Woolf) and Duncan Grant
provided complementarity in their relationship that kept each
other's creative juices flowing: "When Vanessa was timid, Duncan
would be audacious, and when he was disoriented, she would
be authoritative. She would straighten out his muddles and
laugh at his perplexities, and when, as so often happened, her
self-confidence failed her, he would support and reassure her."[10]

A difference in temperament and working style can produce
a level of creativity that is not possible otherwise. Richard Feynman, the brilliant and extraverted physicist, had a partner in the
introverted Freeman Dyson, a young mathematician at Cornell
University. Feynman and Dyson would go on long road trips

together, and Dyson listened patiently to Feynman's imaginative ramblings. He knew what Feynman was creating, and it became his job to "translate Feynman back into the language that other people could understand."[11]

Steve Jobs had a creative partner in Larry Ellison, the founder of Oracle, and vice versa. On a regular basis they would go for long walks to talk and exchange ideas. Ellison explained that his "25-year friendship with Steve was made up of a 1,000 walks."[12] Even as Jobs was dying of cancer, Ellison was there to walk and talk with him. "The walks just kept getting shorter, until near the end we'd just walk around the block."[13] For Ellison, one particular walk stood out—the time in the summer of 1995 when they walked for hours in the Santa Cruz mountains and discussed Steve's desire to return to Apple. The only problem was Apple did not want him, as they had fired him a decade earlier. Since then, Apple had struggled, and Steve felt he needed to be at the helm and talked about the challenges facing the company and various strategic options. Ellison raised the option of buying a majority interest in Apple to provide Jobs with control and both of them with a big financial return. Jobs placed both his hands on Ellison's shoulders, looked him straight in the eye, and said, "I'm not doing this for money. If I do this, I need to do this standing on the high moral ground."[14]

The Jobs-Ellison partnership was a profound relationship that allowed Jobs to explore ideas, try out theories, expand his thinking, and push the boundaries in a way that he could never do walking alone or with regular colleagues.

Creative work is messy work, so you need a collaborator who has a stomach for it and who is not going to flee when the going gets tough or when you are feeling raw and vulnerable. It can be painful at times as you must explore numerous pathways to discover what works, even if that entails going down paths that may turn out to be dead ends. A good partner understands that this is a critical feature of the creative process, and therefore brings patience and persistence to the relationship. They support you in your leadership journey.

Expand Your Moral Capacities

Change agent leadership also requires a healthy dose of moral wisdom. By "moral wisdom" I mean an ethical compass to guide you in figuring out the appropriateness of the change that you seek and the processes you employ as you go about your work. Given the problems generated today by tribalizing authority figures, ugly groups, extremists, corrupt politicians, and irresponsible corporations, there will be times that you must be willing to be a voice against injustice and abuse, even if such a stand puts you at risk. Moral wisdom is needed to determine when to express courage and when to refrain; when a full-frontal attack is needed, and when a paced process of steady adaptation is the best approach.

Expanding your moral capacities requires distinguishing between your personal convictions and moral wisdom. Just because you have a set of convictions does not mean you have moral wisdom, and just because you are willing to take a stand does not mean you are displaying moral courage. Often convictions are the product of your group's cultural narrative, and they may not orient you in the right direction when it comes to successfully dealing with a complex adaptive challenge. Moral wisdom is needed to discern between an inherited "bag of virtues" and what is required to promote the common good.[15] An extremist group, for example, can tap their group's beliefs and values to justify widespread violence—not what all people would regard as contributing to the common good. If "what I believe is right" simply means advancing your tribe's interests over another tribe's, then your actions will likely lack moral wisdom.

My colleague at the Harvard Kennedy School, Ken Winston, who teaches ethics and morality, makes the point that "personal principles, no matter how important or foundational, do not necessarily have a claim on anybody else. Thus, sincerity of conviction is not an acceptable basis of public action."[16] Your convictions can be important in moving you from apathy to action, but they should be subject to scrutiny to see whether they make sense given the problem that you face and the diverse groups connected to the challenge. Leadership can impact the lives of many people; therefore, it is important not to lead from your convictions with the intent of swaying people to your beliefs, but to work with others to ascertain what the common good for that particular context is.

I am not suggesting that as a change agent you should be value neutral. Change is about the promotion of values, particularly as they pertain to inclusivity, fairness, equity, and justice. John Dewey said it best: "A man who starts out on a career of burglary may grow in that direction . . . into a highly expert burglar. Hence it is argued that 'growth' is not enough; we must also specify in which direction growth takes place, and the end toward which it tends."[17]

The work of the change agent is to help a group, or multiple groups, specify what progress might look like, what values lead to progress, and what values impede progress—and the answers might be very different for different groups at different times. Through the process of dialogue, inquiry, and learning through trial and error, groups can make important discoveries. You, as a change agent, might also discover that your own sacred values are flawed or need reinterpreting, and it is you that needs to change!

Moral courage comes from the heart—it seeks to break down barriers, speaks on behalf of being inclusive, not exclusive, and spotlights hypocrisy. An extraordinary example of moral courage can be found in the Grimké sisters.

In the early 1830s, two sisters from South Carolina in the United Sates, Sarah and Angelina Grimké, left their family and friends in the South and moved to the North. They were taking a moral stand against slavery. They lived on a plantation, and their own family had slaves. The sisters found the practice repulsive and, unlike other Southern belles at the time, decided they would sacrifice their good life, even the relationship with their family and friends, and work to end this horrible stain on America.

On Wednesday, February 21, 1838, Angelina Grimké was invited to address the Massachusetts state legislature in Boston on her direct experience as a witness to slavery. The State House was packed, and a large crowd of supporters, curious onlookers, and opponents surrounded the building. This was a time when many Northerners cared little for the battle against slavery, knew very little about the South, and also believed a woman should be at home rather than meddling in political affairs. This is what she said:

> I stand before you as a Southerner, exiled from the land of my birth by the sound of the lash and piteous cry of the slave. I stand before you as a repentant slaveholder. I stand before you as a moral being, and as a moral being I feel that I owe it to the suffering slave and to the deluded master, to my country and to the world to do all that I can to overturn a system of complicated crimes, built upon the broken hearts and prostrate

bodies of my countrymen in chains and cemented by the blood, sweat and tears of my sisters in bonds.[18]

This was a historic moment, as the thirty-three-year-old Grimké was the first woman to ever speak in the State House, and she was also exposing the ugliness of a portion of the country that included her own family. She later recalled, "I was never so near fainting under the tremendous pressure of feeling. My heart almost died within me. The novelty of the scene, the weight of responsibility . . . all together sunk me to the earth. I well nigh despaired."[19] But Grimké did not despair—she found the courage and strength to shake the earth just a little bit on that cold winter's day in Boston.

Moral courage must have moral principles that drive such behavior, and these principles must pertain to the common good, inclusivity, and justice. Many change agents put their lives on the line, so the questions of what is worth fighting for—even dying for—are important questions that demand moral wisdom.

Be a Reflective Practitioner

To expand your boundaries you must be a reflective practitioner, someone that constantly seeks to reflect on their behavior, strategies of action, and intentions.[20] By being more reflective, you are able to make more informed choices, take corrective action, and ensure that your actions are appropriate to the context. Some reflective questions you might ask yourself are as follows:

- How might I be bound up in this problem and complex system in ways that I do not fully realize?
- What action options might be available to me that I have not considered before because of my closeness to the problem?

- For what defensive purpose is my role being used by some groups to avoid doing the adaptive work of change?

Conscious self-reflection is difficult, particularly as it pertains to reflecting on the deeper assumptions that inform one's intentions and behavior, especially when errors are made. People are generally better at seeing other people's errors than their own, and thereby they blame others or factors in the environment and unwittingly absolve themselves from learning and responsibility.[21]

Over the years, I have worked with hundreds of midcareer students at Harvard and had them reflect on a leadership failure in their life. I have noticed a pattern to this learning process: Most people believe the following: that they were not to blame for the failure; their interpretation of the problem was correct; they handled the problem the best way they knew how; their judgment about the features of the problem was fairly accurate and based on valid information; and other people, not themselves, were the primary culprits in the creation of the problem and the failure of leadership.

Upon deeper analysis of their cases, what these students invariably discover is (1) their diagnosis of the problem was flawed, and there were important pieces of information that they missed; (2) their initial judgments about the actors and groups involved were biased and informed by a narrow view of human nature that did not appreciate how complex systems generated interdependent adaptive challenges; (3) their intervention strategies emerged out of a limited range of options and were largely ineffective in producing the desired outcome; and (4) they contributed to the problem in ways that they were unaware of at the time.

To gain such insights can be a powerful learning experience for anyone. However, to gain such insights you must be suspicious of your own mind, constantly interrogating the assumptions under-lying your actions and your beliefs about where the boundaries are and what your role in the system should be.

I once had a student who was a UN official at the time of the Rwandan genocide of 1994 when eight hundred thousand people were killed. By working with his fellow students in the classroom, he was able to engage in a reflective process that allowed him to see how he and his colleagues had made assumptions about the crisis and the actors involved that constrained their capacity to cross bureaucratic, institutional, state, and political boundaries to intervene to end the crisis. He realized that there were other intervention strategies he and others might have pur-sued. At the time, he felt trapped in the bureaucratic and political cultural drift of the UN. He also acknowledged that there was little creativity, responsibility, or cross-boundary leadership from the people, agencies, and governments that could have provided leadership and support. Indeed, President Bill Clinton called his administration's policy on Rwanda the biggest leadership failure of his presidency. Kofi Annan, who was head of peacekeeping operations for Africa at the time, also called Rwanda the greatest failure of his career.[22]

After the fact, and with some distance, it is easier to reflect on breakdowns, errors of judgment, and missed opportunities. Such reflective work is important in order to extract lessons and to ensure that the same errors are not repeated. However, the challenge for anyone seeking to practice leadership is to reflect in real-time in the midst of action when emotions are high, confusion is in the air, and tough choices must be made. Can you reflect on the actors in the system and see the boundaries, constraints, and competing perspectives? Can you see where people are stuck? Can you see where you are stuck or might get stuck? And, when errors are made in judgment or strategy, can you swiftly extract lessons, make midcourse corrections, and reorient yourself?

The human tendency to distance oneself from the responsibility for problems is what I call the *protective stance*. With the protective stance, people distance themselves from learning and responsibility by attributing blame to others, justifying their own position, and believing the problem is too complex or messy to resolve, so it is better to go about their work and play it safe, do nothing, or bypass the hot issues. When individuals deploy this protective stance, they collude in anti-learning behavior, and they may actually exacerbate the problem, as witnessed in Rwanda.

The *learning stance* is about being a reflective practitioner and doing the reflective and detective work of examining your behavior and exploring how the system is reacting to your interventions and to what degree progress on the challenge is being made. The learning stance encourages and promotes creativity, experimentation, and learning from failure. Even though a problem seems intractable, overwhelming, and terribly confusing, when approached from the learning stance, you engage the challenge with curiosity. You actually become a force to be reckoned with because you are tough on yourself and ruthless in your questioning to discover what works, what does not, and what is missing.

In conclusion, it is important to note that wisdom is not an end state. You do not just become a wise person and the job is done. The process of cultivating wisdom and expanding your personal boundaries is about the journey rather than the destination, and it is a lifelong journey. Without the passion for wisdom, you may be a dangerous instrument of power—dangerous to yourself, dangerous to others, and dangerous to the work of change. What is important is that you have a passion for cultivating wisdom through reflection and for pursuing experiences that can enhance your capacity to see the complexity of the system and to see yourself in it, in order to better navigate the system on behalf of leadership and change.

EXPANDING YOUR PERSONAL BOUNDARIES
QUESTIONS FOR PRACTICE

1. Do you have sufficient insight into your own group cultural narrative and appreciate how it informs your behavior?

2. What novel, challenging, and cultural experiences can you participate in to cultivate a more global mindset?

3. Who can you invite to become a boundary-expanding partner?

4. How might you expand your moral sensitivities to ensure they go beyond a "bag of virtues" or dogmatic principles to generate progress for the greater good?

5. To become a reflective practitioner and develop the capacity to examine your own behavior—your actions, values, and assumptions—can you see yourself in the context of the wider system and study your interventions, others' reactions, and the outcomes?

CHAPTER 8

Keeping Yourself from Fracturing

It is easy to feel fractured and burdened when taking on a difficult adaptive challenge. You can internalize the conflicts and frustrations of the groups you are working with, and you can overwhelm yourself by trying to take on too much. At times, you will feel like a lightning rod in the sense of attracting unwanted attention, criticism, adulation, even delusional fantasies that people project onto you. You might get attacked from your own faction because they see you crossing boundaries and partnering with opponents, or you might be criticized by other groups who see you as an irritant, an itinerant, or a serious threat. One can easily become disheartened or cynical, and act out or burn out.

In this final chapter, I present eight important lessons on how to keep yourself from fracturing and find satisfaction and joy in providing leadership.

LESSON 1
You Don't Have to Save the World Today—or Tomorrow

As a change agent, it is easy to become overly responsible for the problem, feeling that you alone have to do it all—fight the battles, be the spokesperson, negotiate, intervene, manage the resources, and fix the problem—*and* do it all today. Committed, passionate people can be like that; they cannot rest until the situation of irresolution is brought to resolution. The consequences, however, can be burnout or a personal breakdown. Consider the case of Jason Russell.

Russell displayed change agent leadership in 2012 in highlighting via the Internet the evils of Joseph Kony and his Lord's Resistance Army in Uganda. However, within a few months, he had a serious mental breakdown and was arrested for running naked through the streets of San Diego, vandalizing cars, and abusing passers-by. He had short-circuited. Why?

Russell was the thirty-three-year-old co-founder of Children International and creator of the twenty-nine-minute YouTube video that explained how Kony and his army wreaked havoc in northern Uganda over two decades by raping, maiming, pillaging, kidnapping, and killing. The public reaction was unprecedented in YouTube's history, as more than a hundred million people viewed the video to learn about Kony's antics. Russell was wielding a new form of cross-boundary leadership by deploying popular media to get the attention of people all over the world.

The response, however, was not all positive. Some groups criticized Russell for presenting a simplistic and outdated view of the problem. One minute he was being lauded as a hero, and then the next minute he was being told he was a low-life, guilty of exploiting the Ugandans for his own personal gain and aggrandizement.

The experience was an emotional roller coaster for which Russell was ill prepared.

On March 15, 2012, Russell had a psychotic breakdown brought on by traveling, speaking, writing, responding, fending off criticisms, and dealing with the pressure of being an overnight celebrity change agent. He later recalled:

> It was so exciting because it felt like the world was for us, and then at the same time it was heartbreaking and felt almost like a nightmare because it felt like the world was against us. . . . My mind couldn't stop thinking about the future—I literally thought I was responsible for the future of humanity. It started to get to the point where my mind finally turned against me and there was a moment that—click, I wasn't in control of my mind or my body.[1]

Most change agents are passionate people who derive from their work existential significance and personal value. Their work gives them meaning. Psychologists have noted that many high-performing people use their work as a substitute for attending to family, friends, and their general well-being.[2] Their job defines them, and they think that they are indispensable and that no one else can do what they do.

Given their zealotry, oftentimes these high-performers are not open to criticism, let alone feedback or support from potential partners. When they experience very demanding predicaments that they cannot resolve or they come face-to-face with failure, they despair and burn out.[3] If they feel there is still so much to do or that they are making little progress, or if they are unable to partner to reduce the load, the stress will increase, particularly when they feel obligated to fix the problem or achieve a specific goal with urgency. Therefore, as a change agent, you must guard against feeling overly responsible because it only adds to the burden that is already overwhelming.

LESSON 2

Surround Yourself with People Who Can Keep You from Doing Stupid Things

To keep your sanity as well as to keep you from getting into trouble, you need good people around you to be a voice of reason and support. These people can lighten the load by carrying the burden and, at times, by carrying you! You need people who are willing to challenge you and to compensate for your blind spots and ensure that your personal hungers do not get in the way. We all have hungers—the hunger for status, power, affiliation, or even grandiosity. If we are too arrogant about our positions and if we cannot contain our hungers, trouble awaits.

One person who did not appreciate this point was Lance Armstrong, the American cyclist. He was not exactly a change agent but certainly someone who used his celebrity as an eight-time Tour de France "winner" to do some good things in the world through the Lance Armstrong Foundation. In 2008, he was considered one of "America's Best Leaders," according to Harvard's Center for Public Leadership and *U.S. News & World Report*.[4] Of course, that was before his fall. In an interview about his leadership, Armstrong said that what was important for him was to have on his team smart, fun, and optimistic people. "I have a very hard time being around pessimism and negativity," he added. "I can't ever imagine walking into a room or a meeting and saying, 'We can't do this.'"[5]

Five years after that statement, Armstrong admitted to a long history of drug cheating, and the sports officials who had once honored him stripped him of all his Olympic medals and seven

Tour de France victories. A hero to the world and a "best leader" for America fell to condemnation as a cheat and liar. While he never wanted people around him who would say "We can't do this," that was exactly the kind of person he needed around him. He needed someone who would say, "Lance, stop it! What you are doing is wrong." Instead, he preferred people who would agree with him, feed his delusions, and collude in his duplicity, all in order to win.

When the people around you reinforce particular tendencies and fail to challenge you, how can you make informed choices that could make a real difference? You do not want people who only agree with you or pander to you. To keep yourself from breaking down or making grave errors, surround yourself with people who are willing to talk straight and tell you the truth, even if that means saying, "You are being a jerk."

LESSON 3
Don't Take It Personally, Even Though It Feels Personal

As a change agent working on a difficult adaptive challenge, it is inevitable that you will become a lightning rod and be struck by occasional criticism and attack from those who see you as a threat. When under attack, it is natural to feel personally affronted and react defensively because you think your motives, integrity, or reputation are being questioned or sullied. A natural reaction might be to respond by "taking up the sword" to fight the offender and to defend your honor. This reaction could be a grave error. You must be able to regulate your emotions.

In the eighteenth century, England's youngest prime minister, William Pitt, was challenged by an opposition member of Parliament to a duel. To defend his honor, Pitt accepted the challenge, and the two men had their shootout at a public park. No one was killed that day. The newspaper joked that the prime minister was so skinny that it was impossible to hit him, and they also suggested that he must be blind because his opponent was too fat to miss.[6] While many people had a good laugh about the incident, Pitt was criticized by his dear friend and parliamentarian William Wilberforce, who impressed upon him the stupidity to risk his life over "honor" when such great issues were at stake for the country.

Wilberforce himself, only a few years earlier, had the captain of a slave ship challenge him to a duel. Wilberforce was the primary advocate in Parliament for ending Britain's involvement in the slave trade. Eventually, due to his valiant change agent leadership in Parliament and throughout the nation, the slave trade was abolished in 1807, fifty-eight years before it ended in the United States. The slave trade was lucrative business for England, so understandably many people saw Wilberforce as a threat and actively criticized and demonized him, with some seeking to kill him. When the slave ship captain challenged him to a duel, Wilberforce declared he would have nothing to do with such nonsense. Wilberforce was no coward, as he was on the front lines of the battle to end slavery. He would not allow himself to get distracted and possibly killed over a trivial offense.[7]

In leading groups to address a difficult adaptive challenge, you must expect a degree of criticism and attack. People will criticize your approach and style, and question your intentions, your actions, your integrity, and your morals. The challenge is to not lash out. Cooler heads need to prevail if you are to stay alive to continue your leadership work.

As a lightning rod, you need to have a degree of what social psychologists call self-complexity. Self-complexity means seeing oneself with many parts, qualities, and roles, rather than as a monolithic self. We all play multiple roles, such as manager, employee, boss, supporter, husband, wife, father, mother, son, and daughter. When you can distinguish between each of the roles you play, you can better manage the pressure and emotional variance that accompanies stressful change work. As a change agent, you must be able to distinguish, as my colleague Ronald Heifetz says, between the self and the role.[8] Attacks can hurt, and the stress can be burdensome, but if you can differentiate roles and move with ease from one role to another, the forces causing stress are buffered and the intensity of the stress is dissipated.

Research on this topic is very clear: under stress, people with high self-complexity experience fewer depressive and physical symptoms than people with low self-complexity.[9] Why? Because low self-complexity may suggest that your notion of self is connected to one particular role; when exposed to a stressful event, you internalize the stress because you have no other roles to help buffer it and displace the burden.

Therefore, refrain from "putting all your eggs in one basket." Do not take troubles in one domain as a reflection of your self-worth or effectiveness in other domains. When people are being critical, disrespectful, or abusive, it is generally because of what you represent and embody for them in the context of the adaptive challenge—not because of who you are as an individual. Although it might seem personal, it really is not personal.

LESSON 4
When the Forces of Darkness Are upon You,
Reconnect to Your Higher Sense of Purpose

To keep yourself from fracturing, you need a strong sense of purpose. Purpose generates resilience and perspective, and keeps your passion burning. Purpose is more than just a good idea or an objective; it is a profound commitment—a commitment that can hold you, anchor you, and orient you. When the challenge is overwhelming, attacks are regular, and success is elusive, it is a natural reaction to think, "Why bother?" Reconnecting with your sense of purpose can help to ensure that your own internal flame of hope is not extinguished. Purpose can give you sufficient energy to continue, even when you feel that you are meandering in circles or only inching forward with little observable progress.

Abraham Lincoln was a purposeful man, but he suffered from serious depression, or "melancholy" as it was known back then.[10] He lived in extremely trying times and, as president, took on three very burdensome but connected challenges: to fight the Civil War, to end slavery, and to mend a broken country. In 1862, in the midst of the war, Lincoln's friend, Senator Orville Browning, dropped by the White House for a quick chat. Browning recorded the visit in his journal, which gives us some insight into the nature of both the burden Lincoln carried and the man himself:

> He was in his library writing. . . . He looked weary, care-worn and troubled. I shook hands with him, and asked how he was. He said "tolerably well." I remarked that I felt concerned about him, regretted that troubles crowded so heavily upon him, and feared his health was suffering. He held me by the hand, pressed it, and said in a very tender and touching tone, "Browning I must die sometime." I replied, "Your fortunes Mr. President are bound up with those of the country, and disaster to one would be disaster to the other, and I hope you will do all you can to preserve your health and life." There was a cadence of deep sadness in his voice. We parted, both of us with tears in our eyes.[11]

Given Lincoln's chronic depression, it is amazing that in such demanding circumstances he was able to contain his suffering, manage his well-being, and provide the leadership needed to orchestrate one of the most profound turning points in American history. Lincoln was the embodiment of being purposeful. Even though depressive by nature, his sense of purpose held him, oriented him, invigorated him, and gave him the passion to do the extraordinary work that he did.

Passion is the indicator that one's sense of purpose is alive and well. If the work is not purposeful, interesting, stimulating, and joyful, then the passion needed might be too weak to keep you in the game. What generates passion and purpose will be different for each person. One thing is sure: without passion and purpose, you will not have enough energy to make a difference. You will eventually peter out.

The Hollywood actor Jim Carrey is a passionate person with a profound sense of purpose. I once spent a week with Carrey in Madagascar. I was the adviser to the president, and Carrey came to visit and offer support through his Better-U Foundation. His focus was primarily on helping farmers with a new form of rice growing that would increase their yields without the use of soil-contaminating fertilizers. But he also brought with him wheelchairs that could be given to people with disabilities. Madagascar is one of the poorest countries in the world, and even the common wheelchair is too costly for most people. The day Carrey was leaving, outside the hotel, he randomly gave one of his wheelchairs to a young man who had been ravaged by polio. An hour later, I got a phone call from Carrey as he was headed for the airport; he was ecstatic. He just had to call and let me know that as he was driving through the town, he saw the fellow to whom he had given the wheelchair, rolling along the street like he was the happiest guy in the world. Carrey couldn't contain himself. He was thrilled! Whether it was seeing a young man use his wheelchair for the first time or noticing a rice shoot emerge through the muddy soil in a remote rural paddy to feed a hungry family, Carrey's passion was obvious and contagious. No wonder Carrey is so purposeful and alive when he gets in front of the cameras in Hollywood—all he has to do is think of that man on his first wheelchair ride rolling happily along the boulevard, and he is inspired!

LESSON 5
Laugh a Lot

Jim Carrey knows something about this next lesson, too. To stay resilient in your attempts to change the world, you should also be able to laugh a lot—at yourself, at the predicament, and about all the "crazy" people and events that you will inevitably encounter on your leadership journey. "The joyous heart is a good remedy, but a crushed spirit dries up the bones," wrote the wise King Solomon.[12]

Larry Ellison, the founder of Oracle, told of how he and Steve Jobs would occasionally go to Kona, Hawaii, with their partners to relax and renew, and Jobs would break out in laughter for no apparent reason, and soon they would both be hysterical. "Those moments are my most cherished and enduring memories of my time with Steve," Ellison reflected, "sitting together at Kona, eating papayas, and laughing for no reason at all."[13]

Humor is essential to keeping your spirit alive. If you take the work of change too seriously, the stress will harm you, even destroy you. A degree of levity helps to dispel some of the heaviness and frustration associated with change. Social science research supports the view that a good dose of humor can protect you physically and mentally from the negative effects of excessive stress.[14]

Humor is also helpful in holding a team together. It is a form of emotional release and group bonding. If you are always serious, forlorn, despondent, and unhappy, then that demeanor fuels an excessively serious, cautious mood among your group, to the point that people might not even want to work with you. Levity and humor lighten the load. Although Abraham Lincoln suffered from depression, when he was around people he could always be counted on for a good story and a joke.[15]

Not all humor is appropriate. Sarcastic, disparaging, aggressive humor is often directed toward people or groups that are disliked, feared, or disdained. This kind of humor is used to express social dominance or superiority, and social psychologists have a name for it: *cavalier humor beliefs*.[16] Cavalier humor might appear to be lighthearted, uncritical, and nonchalant expressions of humor, but researchers have noted that such humor often masks serious biases and prejudice as it can be crude, offensive, and downright nasty. Such humor, in a perverse way, contributes to bonding the in-group while harming the out-group by demeaning or trivializing them. One study found that men who held hostile feelings toward women commonly used sexist humor to make their case.[17] In another study, men exposed to sexist humor became more sexist in their position and, when given the opportunity, chose not to support women's causes.[18] When cavalier humor is used, people become less critical in their thinking and more accepting of the underlying, implicit messages in the humor. Such humor dehumanizes other groups and impedes the work of change.

But other forms of humor are adaptive. *Adaptive humor* is stress-reducing humor that lightens the mood and releases pain, anger, despair, and tension. If it helps people step back and gain perspective, it is congenial and empathetic. The group has a good laugh together, and as they laugh they feel better about themselves, their work, and the mess they are in. It is a form of relief and release. This kind of laughter is a shared cathartic experience that bonds a group and keeps them in the game. The levity is a product of the contrast between pain and possibility, and between the absurdity of the moment and the way things should be. It can be a way of reducing the aversive nature of the situation and helping people to cope with the problem itself. Humorous reactions to stress can increase positive sentiments about the challenge, whereas complaining or wallowing in despair can increase feelings of cynicism and hopelessness.[19]

Humor also allows for a certain degree of distancing from the stressful event, which helps in seeing alternative perspectives and generating creativity.[20] The levity actually promotes objectivity and helps people to see subtlety, nuance, difference, and similarity.

LESSON 6
Start Dancing

When you are frustrated, nobody is listening, and you feel like you have hit a wall and are ready to give up, start dancing. Move from the heavy burden of the challenge to lighter, playful activities to generate a richer human connection with others and a deeper appreciation for the people you are working with and the context in which you operate. "Dancing" in this way can relieve stress, stimulate your imagination, generate partnerships, and produce new options. It can help you get beyond your cynicism or disappointment and create a new space for connection and contribution.

One of my students, Jennifer Hollett, an amazing young woman from Canada, faced a difficult adaptive challenge working in Sierra Leone, Africa. She was there to work at the state media company as a trainer and to support local journalists on a project to address corruption in government and human rights. She struggled to be listened to and accepted by the local people, who related to her as just another foreign consultant intruding into their lives, telling them how bad they were and what they needed to do. With little progress being made, she was ready to give up. But Jennifer loves to dance, so she asked a group of local dancers if she could join their dance group. This opened up a whole new experience for her and an opportunity to connect with people at a level that was not available in the professional sphere. Through the experience of dancing, Jennifer displayed humility and vulnerability in order to be open to what they had to teach, including their feedback and criticism. She was also able to share with them her Western dance moves, adding fun, delight, and some cultural mixing. But most of all, she was able to be a part of a community and to be in their world, on their terms, and simply enjoy a powerful experience of human connection.

Jennifer's experience is an important lesson for anyone crossing boundaries, dealing with fractures, and struggling to provide change agent leadership—join in the dance! I am using the term "join in the dance" figuratively, although in Jennifer's case it was literal. Joining the dance is a multidimensional way of being with people. Sometimes you have to engage informally with others, through casual, fun experiences, and not be so solemn in your change agent role or amid the stress of the adaptive challenge. Joining the dance is a freeing up and renewal process—for you and the group.

LESSON 7
Get Lost—Replenish the Body and the Spirit

Dealing with interdependent problems, you are inadvertently plugged into multiple circuits of groups, issues, and activities. Given the stress and intensity of the work, sometimes the best thing to do to is to get lost—to go away and take a real break. Persistent rumination over a current challenge and anticipation of future problems activates stress-related problems such as the inability to sleep, moodiness, and exhaustion.[21] It can also lead to burnout. To ensure that you can face the challenge with energy and attention, you have to get lost on a regular basis. "Getting lost" means removing yourself from the thick of the challenge and engaging in activities that allow for a totally different sensory experience that has nothing to do with the work of change.[22]

My former student and now dear friend Balu Subramaniam has provided significant leadership to the indigenous tribal peoples of Karnataka in southern India. When he graduated with his medical degree in the 1980s, rather than go to a big city and be a doctor to the rich and make a lot of money, he immediately went to the forest to serve the tribal peoples. He lived with them and immersed himself in their affairs, providing health and medical services, helping them to fight their political battles against the state that was trying to move them off their traditional lands, building schools and hospitals, and adjudicating their disputes. The tribe even made him an honorary chief. To them, he was a hero. The media, too, lauded him as a hero.

But Balu felt empty and burned out. After twenty years of intense service, he was exhausted—mentally, physically, and spiritually—and wondered what he was doing. He had status and he was doing meaningful work, but to what degree was he really making a difference? He went away for two days to meditate at Gandhi's old ashram in Ahmedabad. While there he realized that the tribal peoples were too dependent on him, and he was failing to do the adaptive work of building their capacity to negotiate their development and solve their own problems. He concluded that he was too central in their lives, and it had to become their work, not his.

Balu's next renewal exercise was to take a twenty-eight-day walking journey across the country—traveling 420 kilometers and visiting 120 villages. He did not take any money or food with him but fasted or accepted whatever meal a villager might give him. This journey led to further renewal and the realization that it was time to change his approach to leadership and service. He took time off, went to Harvard for a year, redesigned his life, and planned the next level of his contribution.

You might not be inclined to wander across the country without food or lodging in pursuit of personal wisdom, but you must find the time and space to reflect on the value and meaning of what you are doing. Research indicates that even removing yourself for a short time from problems, such as in the evenings and on weekends, plays a vital role in physical and mental renewal, thwarting the forces that contribute to burnout.[23]

Meditation is another wonderful way to detach when you can't physically remove yourself for a long time. It has certainly helped Aung San Suu Kyi of Burma. In the 1990 general election, her party, the National League for Democracy, won 89 percent of the vote, and she was set to become the president. However, Burma's military junta refused to acknowledge the election result and imprisoned her. She was kept under house arrest until 2009, making her one of the world's most prominent political prisoners. One practice that allowed her to maintain perspective was meditation. "I gained control of my thoughts. It heightens your awareness. If you're aware of what you are doing, you become aware of the pros and cons of each act. That helps you to control not just what you do, but what you think and what you say."[24]

Intermittent renewal is about having a decent break on a regular basis. As human beings we have to have our breaks, or we break down. You have to detach yourself from engagement of the big challenge by distancing yourself from obligations and responsibilities, and doing something totally different and unrelated.[25] Nowadays, however, physically leaving the work environment does not necessarily mean detachment because of the availability of smartphones, laptops, and tablets. What is important is that you are psychologically detached, so that your mental and emotional space is being filled with stimuli and sensations unrelated to work.

One study found that although the effects of burnout subsided during a vacation, they actually returned to the pre-vacation levels three weeks after the vacation![26] This would suggest that one cannot rely exclusively on the big break as the source of replenishment. You need to consciously be engaged in both daily and intermittent renewal of your spirit, mind, and body—or else you will burn out and be unable to provide the quality of leadership needed to make a genuine and powerful contribution.

LESSON 8

Choose Your Battles Wisely, and Know When to Walk Away

One of the most common and dangerous risks for anyone seeking to provide leadership lies in fighting battles: fighting the wrong battle, fighting the right battle in the wrong way, or not knowing when to stop fighting the battle and walk away. No other aspect of leadership calls for greater wisdom. You should maintain a clear-eyed, sober appreciation of the consequences of battle for yourself, your people, and the groups you battle with. If you are unwise pertaining to the battles of change, you might lose your health, your job, or your life, thus jeopardizing the work of change.

On the one hand, all of us can agree that some things are simply not worth fighting for. On the other hand, some things *are* worth fighting for—even at a very high cost. Gandhi knew he had to undertake a moral battle against British rule; Martin Luther King knew he had to fight against racism and bigotry. Indeed, many battles will need to be waged if organizations, schools, communities, and nations are to face hard realities, deal responsibly with their problems, and pave a pathway forward that generates real progress. But knowing what battles need to be fought and how to fight those battles with wisdom is the challenge of leadership. The American president Woodrow Wilson, who held office in the early twentieth century, is a great example of someone who lacked this wisdom when it was most needed.

President Wilson went to battle with Congress in order to create the conditions and institutions that could end all war. As president during World War I, he had sent more than one hundred thousand young American men to die in battle. He was committed that such a war should never be fought again. He knew that without radical political changes pertaining to how nations interacted to solve their problems, humans might well annihilate themselves. His solution to this problem was support for the newly created League of Nations, and his challenge was to get the United States to join.

Wilson's fight to get the American people to support the League was one of the most significant political battles of the twentieth century. Many Americans did not want to join the League. They did not want to get entangled in European politics, disputes, or wars; therefore, the Republican Congress refused to support Wilson in his quest—not without compromise, at least.[27] Wilson, however, refused to compromise. "I have found one can never get anything in this life that is worthwhile without fighting for it," he said.[28] This bulldog-like attitude brought him down. He appeared to the nation, one historian wrote, "as a self-righteous, impractical idealist who committed infanticide on his own cherished creation, rather than bend in the face of an unavoidable reality."[29] Nearly every League advocate was willing to accept reservations and amendments, as they saw it as being better than nothing—but not Woodrow Wilson.

After failing to succeed with Congress, Wilson went directly to the American people. But the political battles in Washington had exhausted him. As he began his national speaking tour, his doctor told him he was in no physical condition to take on such an arduous task. Nevertheless, the president embarked on a twenty-one-day train trip across the country, making more than forty speeches and granting dozens of interviews. It took its toll: he became physically and emotionally weary, and suffered from constant headaches, asthma attacks, and bouts of depression. Halfway through the tour, his doctor demanded that Wilson cease immediately and return home. The president stubbornly argued with the doctor but then confessed, "I don't seem to realize it, but I have gone to pieces. The doctor is right. I am not in a condition to go on." Wilson then looked out the window and broke down in tears.[30] That night the Wilson "League of Nations train" suddenly turned around and rushed back to Washington.

On March 19, 1920, the Senate made its last vote on the ratification of the League bill. It was defeated. Wilson commented a few days later, "I have given my vitality, almost my life, for the League of Nations, and I would rather lead a fight for the League and lose both my reputation and my life rather than shirk a duty of this kind."[31] Although still in office, Wilson retreated to his bedroom, rarely meeting with people, and the following year he died.

For two years, Wilson had worked tirelessly to achieve his goal, only to fail in the end. The United States never did enter into the League of Nations, although the work that he did laid the foundation for the creation of the United Nations more than twenty years later, after another bitter and devastating war. Wilson may well have been right in believing that the battle for the League was worth fighting, but his wisdom deserted him when it came to choosing how and where to fight it, and staking his entire strategy on an all-or-nothing victory. Wilson made the battle for the League of Nations his personal battle. He turned it into a moral crusade.

The battle must never be your battle. It has to be the group's battle. The leadership task is to orchestrate the battle in such a way that people are able to grapple with the implications of their choices and examine the values that orient them in a particular direction. Wilson's battle was, at some level, a noble and selfless fight. Yet, because it was not at all clear that the American people saw it as *their* battle, it was also foolhardy. Had Wilson built an understanding among the people of what was at stake and helped them envision the kind of world they wanted to live in, and what America's role in that world should be, he might have made greater progress. Brilliant, articulate, and deeply moral, Wilson still ignored the principles of choosing your battle wisely, pacing yourself and pacing the work of change, and knowing when to walk away—and he suffered the consequences.

No matter how much you contribute, there will come a time when your personal leadership challenge is to let go and walk away. If you persist, you might hurt yourself, hurt the work, or hurt your partners. An important question you must consider is under what circumstances is it wise to compormise now, walk away from your leadership work, shelve the issue until a later date, or perhaps pass the baton to others?

Exercising leadership as a global change agent is full of dangers and surprises. It is an adventure. The process should be appreciated for what it reveals about yourself, human nature, and the human spirit. The joy is in the experience. Even if you do not get to your destination, cherish the fact that you traversed out into unchartered territory and did the best you could. When it comes time for you to let go, let go with dignity and be calm in the realization that this is how our universe works—not in accord with our personal desires or demands, but with its own indifference and unpredictable twists and turns.

KEEPING YOURSELF FROM FRACTURING
QUESTIONS FOR PRACTICE

1. You don't have to save the world today, or tomorrow. How can you keep yourself from becoming a crusader? Do you have a long-term perspective, and can you pace yourself and pace the work of change?

2. Do you have friends and partners around you who can talk straight and keep you from doing stupid things?

3. When criticized or under attack, do you have the resilience and capacity to not take it personally, stay calm, and respond strategically?

4. When the forces of darkness are upon you and you feel like giving up, how might you reconnect to your higher sense of purpose and maintain your passion?

5. Can you laugh easily—at yourself, at your predicament—as a way to de-stress and maintain perspective?

6. Start dancing! How might you interact with others informally and playfully to connect with people at a more real and human level?

7. Given the burden of responsibility, how can you go about renewal and replenishment of the spirit, body, and mind so that you can be totally present to the work of change and find satisfaction in the work?

8. How can you ensure you are choosing your battles wisely? How can you make it the people's battle and not your personal battle? And under what circumstances do you think it is wise to walk away from your leadership work, postpone it to another day, and perhaps to pass the baton to others?

Notes

Preface

1. R. Heifetz and R. Sinder, "Political Leadership: Managing the Public's Problem Solving," pp. 179–204 in R. Reich (Ed.), *The Power of Public Ideas* (Cambridge, MA: Harvard University Press, 1988).

Chapter 1

1. For the distinction between leadership and authority, see Ronald Heifetz, *Leadership Without Easy Answers* (Cambridge: Harvard University Press, 1994).
2. E. O. Wilson, *The Social Conquest of the Earth* (New York: Liveright, 2013).
3. Joshua Greene, *Moral Tribes: Emotion, Reason, and the Gap Between Us and Them* (New York: Penguin, 2013).
4. Philip Blenkinsop and Robert-Jan Bartunek, "Flemish Separatists Are Big Winners in Belgian Election," *Reuters.com*, U.S. edition, May 25, 2014, www.reuters.com/article/2014/05/25/us-belgium-election-idUSBREA4O0DT20140525.
5. Gordon Brown, *Beyond the Crash: Overcoming the First Crisis of Globalization* (New York: Free Press, 2010), pp. 5, 6.
6. Brown, *Beyond the Crash*, p. 79.

7. Kiyoshi Kurokawa, chairman of the Japan Parliamentary Report; see Hiroku Tabuchi, "Inquiry Declares Fukushima Crisis a Man-Made Disaster," *New York Times*, July 6, 2012, www.nytimes.com/2012/07/06/world/asia/fukushima-nuclear-crisis-a-man-made-disaster-report-says.html?_r=0.

8. Tabuchi, "Inquiry Declares."

9. Lawrence G. McDonald, with Patrick Robinson, *A Colossal Failure of Common Sense: The Inside Story of the Collapse of Lehman Brothers* (New York: Crown, 2010).

10. See Fuld's leadership principles at http://knowledge.wharton.upenn.edu/article/ceo-richard-fuld-on-lehman-brothers-evolution-from-internal-turmoil-to-teamwork/.

11. Edmund L. Andrews, "Greenspan Concedes Error on Regulation," *New York Times*, October 24, 2008, p. B1.

12. Congressional hearing, October 23, 2008.

13. Vikas Bajaj and Michael M. Grynbaum, "For Stocks, Worst Single-Day Drop in Two Decades," *New York Times*, September 30, 2008, p. A1, www.nytimes.com/2008/09/30/business/30markets.html?pagewanted=all&_r=0.

14. Chris Gentilviso, "Gingrich Hits CNN over Its 'Selective Media Outrage' Against Ted Nugent," *Huffington Post*, February 19, 2009, www.huffingtonpost.com/2014/02/19/newt-gingrich-cnn-ted-nugent_n_4815042.html.

15. Treasury Secretary Paul H. O'Neill, "Caring Greatly and Succeeding Greatly: Producing Results in Africa," remarks to the Carnegie Endowment for Peace, Washington, DC, June 5, 2002.

16. Declan Walsh, "How Africa Changed a Powerful Odd Couple on a Tour of the Poor," *New Zealand Herald*, June 3, 2002.

17. Moises Naim, *The End of Power: From Boardrooms to Battlefields and Churches to States, Why Being in Charge Isn't What It Used to Be* (New York: Basic Books, 2013), p. 106.

18. Rosa Parks, *My Story* (New York: Dial Books, 1992).

19. See Josephine Dallant, "How Jokowi Helped Jakarta," *Huffington Post*, www.huffingtonpost.com/josephine-dallant/how-jokowi-helped-jakarta_b_5597421.html.

Chapter 2

1. I first spoke about zooming in and zooming out with my coauthor Riley Sinder in our chapter on "Leadership Styles" in *Clinical Laboratory Management*, ed. L. Garcia (Washington, DC: ASM Press, 2004), pp. 195–210. Rosabeth Moss Kanter also used this concept in the *Harvard Business Review* article "Managing Yourself: Zoom In, Zoom Out" (March 2011).

2. This story was discussed at length in the CBC television program *The National*, airing on July 2, 1992, and available as "Cod Fishing: 'The Biggest Layoff in Canadian History,'" at www.cbc.ca/archives/categories/economy-business/natural-resources/fished-out-the-rise-and-fall-of-the-cod-fishery/the-biggest-layoff-in-canadian-history.html.

3. Greenpeace summarizes this story in its May 8, 2009, piece, "The Collapse of the Canadian Newfoundland Cod Industry," www.greenpeace.org/international/en/campaigns/oceans/seafood/understanding-the-problem/overfishing-history/cod-fishery-canadian/.

4. CBC, "Cod Fishing."

5. J. Marguc, J. Förster, and G. A. Van Kleef, "Stepping Back to See the Big Picture: When Obstacles Elicit Global Processing," *Journal of Personality and Social Psychology* 101, no. 5 (November 2011): 883–901.

6. See the clear description of ocean currents on the website for the Capital Regional District of British Columbia: www.crd.bc.ca/education/our-environment/geology-processes/global-ocean-currents.

7. See Edward Lorenz, *The Edge of Chaos* (Seattle: University of Washington Press), 1993.

8. Clifford Geertz, *The Interpretation of Cultures* (New York: Basic Books, 2005), p. 5.
9. The so-called Gazimestan speech delivered by Milošević is fully explored at http://en.wikipedia.org/wiki/Gazimestan_speech.

Chapter 3

1. Richard Whitmire, *The Bee Eater: Michelle Rhee Takes on the Nation's Worst School District* (San Francisco: Josey-Bass, 2011), p. 69.
2. Michelle Rhee, *Radical: Fighting to Put Students First* (New York: Harper, 2013), Kindle edition, p. 117.
3. Amanda Ripley, "How to Fix America's Schools," *Time*, November 26, 2008.
4. Rhee, *Radical*, p. 177.
5. Rhee, *Radical*, pp. 160–161.
6. Boris Bizumic, John Duckitt, Dragan Popadic, Vincent Dru, and Stephen Krauss, "A Cross-cultural Investigation into a Reconceptualization of Ethnocentrism," *European Journal of Social Psychology* 39, no. 6 (October 2009): 871–899.
7. See Ray A. Moore and Donald L. Robinson, *Partners for Democracy: Crafting the New Japanese State Under MacArthur* (Oxford: Oxford University Press, 2004).
8. PBS has captured MacArthur's "Old Soldiers Never Die" speech to Congress on April 19, 1951, on its website at www.pbs.org/wgbh/amex/macarthur/filmmore/reference/primary/macspeech05.html.
9. Robert Coles, *Lives of Moral Leadership* (New York: Random House, 2000), p. 21.
10. Coles, *Lives of Moral Leadership*, p. 11.
11. Coles, *Lives of Moral Leadership*, p. 15.
12. See Clay Risen, "The Lightning Rod," *The Atlantic*, November 2008, www.theatlantic.com/magazine/archive/2008/11/the-lightning-rod/307058/.
13. Rhee, *Radical*, p. 134.

14. Letter from Marion Barry to Mayor Adrian Fenty, November 28, 2007; see www.dcpswatch.com/mayor/071128.htm.

15. Whitmire, *The Bee Eater*, p. 204.

16. Robert McNamara and James Blight, *Wilson's Ghost: Reducing the Risk of Conflict, Killing, and Catastrophe in the 21st Century* (New York: Public Affairs, 2001), p. 145.

17. For an analysis of the relationship between Vieira de Mello and Bremer, see Samantha Power's book *Chasing the Flame: One Man's Fight to Save the World* (New York: Penguin Books, 2008).

18. Power, *Chasing the Flame*, p. 424.

19. For an appreciation of the complexity of the problems Paul Bremer faced, read his book *My Year in Iraq: The Struggle to Build a Future of Hope* (New York: Threshold Editions, 2006).

20. For insight into how Bremer approached this challenge of dealing with the Ba'athists, see *My Year in Iraq*.

21. Colin Powell, "Colin Powell on the Bush Administration's Iraq War Mistakes," *Newsweek*, May 13, 2012, www.newsweek.com/colin-powell-bush-administrations-iraq-war-mistakes-65023.

22. Evan Thomas, "The Battle over School Reform: Rhee vs. Weingarten," *Newsweek*, March 5, 2010, www.newsweek.com/battle-over-school-reform-rhee-vs-weingarten-69465.

23. See "Murder Comes Naturally to Chimpanzees," www.bbc.com/news/science-environment-29237276.

Chapter 4

1. Jared Diamond, *Collapse: How Societies Choose to Succeed or Fail* (New York: Penguin Books, 2005).

2. Niall Ferguson, "Complexity and Collapse: Empires on the Edge of Chaos," *Foreign Affairs*, March/April 2010, pp. 18–32.

3. Mark J. Perry, "Carpe Diem" blog, http://mjperry.blogspot.com/2011/11/fortune-500-firms-in-1955-vs-2011-87.html.

4. Anton R. Valukas, *Report to Board of Directors of General Motors Company Regarding Ignition Switch Recalls*, May 29, 2014, available from

the *New York Times* at www.nytimes.com/interactive/2014/06/05/business/06gm-report-doc.html?_r=0.

5. Valukas, *Report.*

6. Ben Geier, "GM's CEO Tells Congress: 'I Will Not Rest Until These Problems Are Resolved,'" *Fortune,* June 18, 2014, http://fortune.com/2014/06/18/barra-focuses-testimony-on-gm-changes/.

7. See "Transcript of Julia Gillard's Speech," *Sydney Morning Herald,* October 10, 2012, www.smh.com.au/opinion/political-news/transcript-of-julia-gillards-speech-20121010-27c36.html.

8. Alison Rourke, "Julia Gillard's Attack on Sexism Hailed as a Turning Point for Women," as reported in *The Guardian,* October 12, 2012.

9. See the Invisible Children's video at www.youtube.com/watch?v=Y4MnpzG5Sqc.

10. William Shakespeare, *A Midsummer's Night Dream,* Act V, Scene 1, in *The Plays and Sonnets: Volume 1* (Chicago: Encyclopaedia Britannica, 1990).

11. Karl Weick, "Reflections: Change Agents as Poets—On Reconnecting Flux and Hunches," *Journal of Change Management* 11, no. 1 (March 2011): 7–20.

12. J. Jost, M. Banaji, and B. Nosek, "A Decade of System Justification Theory," *Political Psychology* 25, no. 6 (2004): 881–919.

13. A. Kay, D. Gaucher, J. Peach, K. Laurin, J. Friesen, M. Zanner, and S. Spencer, "Inequality, Discrimination, and the Power of the Status Quo: Direct Evidence for a Motivation to See the Way Things Are as the Way They Should Be," *Journal of Personality and Social Psychology* 97, no. 3 (2009): 421–434.

14. See, for example, W. Beasley, *The Meiji Restoration* (Stanford, CA: Stanford University Press, 1972).

15. "Women's Rights from Past to Present: The Meiji Reforms and Obstacles for Women Japan, 1878–1927," in Women in World History Curriculum, www.womeninworldhistory.com/WR-04.html.

16. Sharon Sievers, *Flowers in Salt: The Beginnings of Feminist Consciousness in Modern Japan* (Stanford, CA: Stanford University Press, 1983).

17. Sievers, *Flowers in Salt*.

18. "Daughters in Boxes" translated by Rebecca Copeland and Aiko Okamoto MacPhail in Rebecca Copeland and Melek Ortabasi, *The Modern Murasaki: Writing of Women in Meiji Japan* (New York: Columbia University Press, 2012).

19. Sievers, *Flowers in Salt*.

20. See http://en.wikipedia.org/wiki/2011_Indian_anti-corruption_movement.

21. I interviewed Srđja Popović on November 30, 2012.

22. Gary Hamel, "Waking Up IBM: How a Gang of Unlikely Rebels Transformed Big Blue," *Harvard Business Review*, July–August 2000, p. 138.

23. Stephen Cohen, *Failed Crusade: America and the Tragedy of Post-Communist Russia* (New York: Norton, 2000).

24. Ezra Vogel, *Deng Xiaoping and the Transformation of China* (Cambridge, MA: Belknap Press, 2011).

25. Bill Turque, "Rhee Says She May Have Tried to Do Too Much Too Soon to Revamp D.C. Schools," *Washington Post*, March 14, 2009, www.washingtonpost.com/wp-dyn/content/article/2009/03/13/AR2009031303270.html.

Chapter 5

1. See www.nasa.gov/exploration/whyweexplore/why_we_explore_main.html.

2. J. R. R. Tolkien, *The Fellowship of the Ring* (Boston: Houghton Mifflin, 2012), Kindle edition, 1650–1651.

3. Hiroshi Mikitani, *Marketplace 3.0: Rewriting the Rules of Borderless Business* (London: Palgrave Macmillan, 2013), Kindle edition, pp. 123–125.

4. "Rakuten's Decision on English Not Welcomed by Everyone," *Japan Today*, www.japantoday.com/smartphone/view/kuchikomi/rakutens-decision-on-english-not-welcomed-by-everyone.

5. Mikitani, *Marketplace 3.0*, 526–528.

6. See www.forbes.com/companies/rakuten/.

7. See www.etymonline.com/index.php?term=fail.

8. Andy Goldsworthy in the documentary *Rivers and Tides*, 2002, directed by Thomas Riedelsheimer.

9. David LeGesse, "America's Best Leaders: Jeff Bezos, Amazon .com CEO," *U.S. News & World Report*, November 19, 2008, www.usnews.com/news/best-leaders/articles/2008/11/19/americas-best-leaders-jeff-bezos-amazoncom-ceo.

10. Chris Argyris, "Teaching Smart People to Learn," *Harvard Business Review*, May 1991.

11. K. W. Phillips, S. Y. Kim-Jun, and S. Shim, "The Value of Diversity in Organizations: A Social Psychological Perspective," pp. 253–272 in *Social Psychology and Organizations*, ed. R. van Dick and K. Murnighan (New York: Routledge, 2010).

12. See "The Anthropology of Innovation" on www.youtube.com/watch?v=BhF0D6NR3l8.

13. Natasha Singer, "Intel's Sharp-Eyed Social Scientist," *New York Times*, February 16, 2014, www.nytimes.com/2014/02/16/technology/intels-sharp-eyed-social-scientist.

14. See, for example, Mihaly Csikszentmihalyi, *Creativity: Flow and the Psychology of Discovery and Invention* (New York: Harper-Collins, 2009).

15. For the contribution of alchemy to modern chemistry, see Matthew D. Eddy, Seymour H. Mauskopf, and William R. Newman, editors, *Chemical Knowledge in the Early Modern World* (Chicago: University of Chicago Press, 2014); see also Carl Zimmer, *Soul Made Flesh: The Discovery of the Brain—and How It Changed the World* (New York: Free Press, 2003).

16. A. C. Homan, J. R. Hollenbeck, S. E. Humphrey, D. van Knippen- berg, D. R. Ilgen, and G. A. van Kleef, "Facing Differences with an Open Mind: Openness to Experience, Salience of Intra-group Differences, and Performance of Diverse Work Groups," *Academy of Management Journal* 51, no. 6 (January 2008): 1204–1222.

17. Doris Kearns Goodwin, *Team of Rivals: The Political Genius of Abraham Lincoln* (New York: Simon & Schuster, 2006).

18. Katerina Bezrukova, Sherry M. B. Thatcher, Karen A. Jehn, and Chester S. Spell, "The Effects of Alignments: Examining Group Faultlines, Organizational Cultures, and Performance," *Journal of Applied Psychology* 97, no. 1 (2012): 77–92.

19. M. S. Granovetter, "The Strength of Weak Ties," *American Journal of Sociology* 78 (1973): 1360–1380.

20. J. Zhou, S. J. Shin, F. J. Brass, J. Choi, and Z.-X. Zhang, "Social Networks, Personal Values, and Creativity: Evidence for Curvi- linear and Interaction Effects," *Journal of Applied Psychology* 94 (2009): 1544–1552.

21. J. E. Perry-Smith, "Social yet Creative: The Role of Social Relation- ships in Facilitating Individual Creativity," *Academy of Management Journal* 49 (2006): 85–101.

22. Zhou et al., "Social Networks."

23. M. Baer, "The Strength-of-Weak-Ties Perspective on Creativity: A Comprehensive Examination and Extension," *Journal of Applied Psychology* 95, no. 3 (May 2010): 592–601.

24. Ed Catmull, "How Pixar Fosters Collective Creativity," *Harvard Business Review* 86 (September 2008): 64–72.

25. Jerry Hirshberg, *The Creative Priority: Driving Innovation in the Real World* (New York: HarperBusiness, 1998), p. 30.

26. Frank R. C. de Wit, Lindred L. Greer, and Karen A. Jehn, "The Paradox of Intragroup Conflict: A Meta-Analysis," *Journal of Applied Psychology* 97, no. 2 (2012): 360–390.

27. John Dewey, *How We Think* (Mineola, NY: Dover, 1910; reprint 1997).

28. Friedrich Schiller, *On the Aesthetic Education of Man in a Series of Letters*, ed. and trans. Elizabeth M. Wilkinson and L. A. Willoughby (Oxford: Clarendon, 1967), p. 107.
29. Schiller, "Letters."
30. Doris Sommer, *The Work of Art in the World: Civic Agency and Public Humanities* (Durham, NC: Duke University Press, 2014).
31. Walter Isaacson, "The Real Leadership Lessons of Steve Jobs," *Harvard Business Review* 90, no. 4 (April 2012): 92–102.
32. For more information on Doris Sommer and her work, see www.culturalagents.org.
33. Antanas Mockus, "Co-Existence as Harmonization of Law, Morality and Culture," *Prospects* 32, no. 1 (March 2002): 19–37.
34. Rollo May, *The Courage to Create* (New York: Norton, 1994).

Chapter 6

1. Boutros Boutros-Ghali, *Unvanquished: A U.S.-U.N. Saga* (New York: Random House, 1999), p. 177.
2. S. Altran and R. Axelrod, "Reframing Sacred Values," *Negotiation Journal* 24, no. 3 (July 2008): 221–246.
3. Tim Phillips, "In Gun Control Debate, Sacred Values Are Often Forgotten," *Global Post*, January 8, 2014.
4. David A. DeVoss, "Ping-Pong Diplomacy," *Smithsonian*, April 2002, www.smithsonianmag.com/history/ping-pong-diplomacy-60307544/?no-ist.
5. PBS, "Ping-Pong Diplomacy (April 6–17, 1971)," *American Experience*, www.pbs.org/wgbh/amex/china/peopleevents/pande07.html.
6. Richard Nixon, "Remarks at Andrews Air Force Base on Returning from the People's Republic of China, February 28, 1972," available through the American Presidency Project, www.presidency.ucsb.edu/ws/?pid=3756.
7. Gordon Allport, *The Nature of Prejudice* (Cambridge, MA: Perseus Books, 1954).

8. T. Pettigrew, "Intergroup Contact Theory," *Annual Review of Psychology* 49, no. 1 (1998): 65–85.

9. The term "discuss the undiscussable" comes from Chris Argyris. See his book *Reasoning, Learning, and Action* (San Francisco: Jossey-Bass, 1982).

10. Chris Argyris, the father of action science, originally termed this "the ladder of inference." See Argyris, *Overcoming Organizational Defenses: Facilitating Organizational Learning* (Needham, MA: Allyn & Bacon, 1990).

11. *Black Harvest*, a documentary by Robert Connolly and Robin Anderson, 1992.

12. Carter related this experience in his Sadat Lecture for Peace at the University of Maryland, October 25, 1998; the transcript of that speech is available through the Anwar Sadat Chair for Peace and Development website: http://sadat.umd.edu/lecture/lecture/carter.htm.

13. Carter, Sadat Lecture for Peace.

14. Emile Bruneau and Rebecca Saxe, "The Power of Being Heard: The Benefits of 'Perspective-Giving' in the Context of Intergroup Conflict," *Journal of Experimental Social Psychology* 48 (2012): 855–866.

15. L. Van Boren, G. Loewenstein, D. Dunning, and L. Nordgren, "Changing Places: A Dual Judgment Model of Empathy Gaps in Emotional Perspective Taking," *Advances in Experimental Psychology* 48 (2013): 117–171.

16. Bruneau and Saxe, "The Power of Being Heard."

17. Altran and Axelrod, "Reframing Sacred Values."

18. David K. Shipler, "Robert McNamara and the Ghosts of Vietnam," *New York Times Magazine*, August 10, 1997, www.nytimes.com/1997/08/10/magazine/robert-mcnamara-and-the-ghosts-of-vietnam.html.

19. From the film *The Fog of War: Eleven Lessons from the Life of Robert S. McNamara*; the transcript is available at www.errolmorris.com/film/fow_transcript.html.

20. Robert S. McNamara, *In Retrospect: The Tragedy and Lessons from Vietnam* (New York: Vintage Books, 1996), p. xx.

21. A. S. Goldman and F. C. Schmalstieg Jr., "Abraham Lincoln's Gettysburg Illness," *Journal of Medical Biography* 15, no. 2 (May 2007): 104–110, www.ncbi.nlm.nih.gov/pubmed/17551612.

22. Garry Wills, *Lincoln at Gettysburg: The Words That Remade America* (New York: Simon & Schuster, 2006).

23. S. L. Gaertner, J. F. Dovidio, P. A. Anastasio, B. A. Bachman, and M. C. Rust, "The Common Ingroup Identity Model: Recategorization and the Reduction of Intergroup Bias," *European Review of Social Psychology* 4, no. 1 (1993): 1–26.

24. Mick Krever, "François Pienaar on Seeing Mandela Wear His Springbok Rugby Jersey," *Amanpour* blog, CNN.com, December 10, 2013, http://amanpour.blogs.cnn.com/2013/12/10/francois-pienaar-on-seeing-mandela-wearing-his-springbok-rugby-jersey-i-bit-my-lip-so-hard-i-wanted-to-cry/.

25. Joseph Montville, "The Healing Function in Political Conflict Resolution," in *Conflict Resolution Theory and Practice: Integration and Application*, ed. Dennis J. D. Sandole and Hugo van der Merwe (New York: Manchester University Press, 1993).

26. M. Wohl, M. Hornsey, and S. Bennett, "When Group Apologies Succeed and Fail: Intergroup Forgiveness and the Role of Primary and Secondary Emotions," *Journal of Personality and Social Psychology* 102, no. 2 (2012): 306–322.

27. See the Australian government's website at http://australia.gov.au/about-australia/our-country/our-people/apology-to-australias-indigenous-peoples.

28. Howard Zehr, *Changing Lenses: A New Focus for Crime and Justice* (Scottsdale, PA: Herald Books, 2005), 268–269.

29. Nikola Luksic, "Rwanda Genocide: Why Jean Paul Samputu Forgives His Family's Murderer," Canadian Broadcasting Company, April 9, 2014, www.cbc.ca/news/world/rwanda-genocide-why-jean-paul-samputu-forgives-his-family-s-murderer-1.2594490.

30. Tom Geoghegan, "Why Do People Still Fly the Confederate Flag?" *BBC News*, Washington, August 29, 2013, www.bbc.com/news/magazine-23705803.

31. Kelly Avellino, "Group Flies 2nd Massive Confederate Flag by I-95 in VA," NBC News Channel 12 affiliate in Richmond, Virginia, June 1, 2014, www.nbc12.com/story/25663862/kelly-tba.

32. Reuters, "Singapore Angry at Indonesia Move to Name Navy Ship for Convicted Bombers," February 7, 2014, www.reuters.com/article/2014/02/07/us-singapore-indonesia-ships.

33. Zakir Hussein and Zubaidah Nazeer, "Straits Times: Indonesia 'Meant No Ill Will' in Naming of Ship," Ministry of Foreign Affairs, Singapore Headlines, www.mfa.gov.sg/content/mfa/media_centre/singapore_headlines/2014/201402/headlines_20140212.html.

Chapter 7

1. Andrew Higgins, Andrew E. Kramer, and Steven Erlangerfeb, "As His Fortunes Fell in Ukraine, a President Clung to Illusions," *New York Times*, February 23, 2014, www.nytimes.com/2014/02/24/world/europe/as-his-fortunes-fell-in-ukraine-a-president-clung-to-illusions.html.

2. *Wall Street Journal* interview, May 30, 2012; see www.youtube.com/watch?v=j-Yk4k2tG4A.

3. For an overview of research on the global mindset, see Joanna Story, "A Developmental Approach to a Global Mindset," *Journal of International Leadership Studies* 6, no. 3 (2011): 375–389; and A. K. Gupta and V. Govindarajan, "Cultivating a Global Mindset," *Academy of Management Executive* 16, no. 1 (2002): 116–126.

4. My notions of complex thinking and the global mindset have been informed by Robert Kegan. See Robert Keegan, *In over Our Heads: The Mental Demands of Modern Life* (Cambridge, MA: Harvard University Press, 1998).

5. Darcia Narvaez and Patrick L. Hill, "The Relation of Multicultural Experiences to Moral Judgment and Mindsets," *Journal of Diversity in Higher Education* 3, no. 1 (2010): 43–55.

6. L. Endicott, T. Bock, and D. Narvaez, "Moral Reasoning, Intercultural Development, and Multicultural Experiences: Relations and Cognitive Underpinnings," *International Journal of Intercultural Relations* 27 (2003): 403–419.

7. Eugene T. Parker III and Ernest T. Pascarella, "Effects of Diversity Experiences on Socially Responsible Leadership over Four Years of College," *Journal of Diversity in Higher Education* 6, no. 4 (2013): 219–230.

8. Gillian Tett, anthropologist, author, and journalist for the *Financial Times*.

9. Vera John-Steiner, *Creative Collaboration* (Oxford: Oxford University Press, 2006).

10. John-Steiner, *Creative Collaboration*, p. 16.

11. John-Steiner, *Creative Collaboration*, p. 47.

12. Alexander Wolfe, "Ellison Honors Jobs at Business Hall of Fame," *Forbes*, November 15, 2013, www.forbes.com/sites/oracle/2013/11/15/ellison-honors-steve-jobs-at-business-hall-of-fame/.

13. Charlie Rose interview with Larry Ellison, August, 14, 2013, www.charlierose.com/watch/60254508.

14. Wolfe, "Ellison Honors Jobs."

15. Lawrence Kohlberg, *The Philosophy of Moral Development: Moral Stages and the Idea of Justice* (New York: Harper & Row, 1981), p. 39.

16. Ken Winston, *Moral Competence in Public Life*, Occasional Paper No. 4 (Victoria, Australia: Australia and New Zealand School of Government, April 2010), www.anzsog.edu.au/media/upload/publication/18_occpaper_04_winston.pdf.

17. Kohlberg, *The Philosophy of Moral Development*, p. 72.

18. Gerda Lerner, *The Grimké Sisters from South Carolina: Pioneers for Women's Rights and Abolition* (Raleigh: University of North Carolina Press, 2004), p. 8.
19. Lerner, *The Grimké Sisters*, p. 5.
20. See Donald A. Schön, *The Reflective Practitioner: How Professionals Think in Action* (New York: Basic Books, 1984).
21. See Chris Argyris, *Reasoning, Learning, and Action* (San Francisco: Jossey-Bass, 1982).
22. See the PBS documentary *Ghosts of Rwanda*. It can be accessed at www.pbs.org/wgbh/pages/frontline/shows/ghosts/.

Chapter 8
1. Russell made these remarks on the television show *Today*, October 8, 2012.
2. H. Freudenberger, *Burn-out: The High Cost of High Achievement* (Garden City, NY: Doubleday, 1980).
3. H. Fischer, "A Psychoanalytic View of Burnout," pp. 40–45 in *Stress and Burnout in the Human Service Professions*, ed. B. Farber (New York: Pergamon Press, 1983).
4. *U.S. News & World Report*, "America's Best Leaders," December 1–8, 2008. The list was formulated by surveys conducted by the center for Public Leadership at Harvard Kennedy School.
5. *U.S. News & World Report*, "America's Best Leaders," p. 53.
6. Kevin Belmonte, *William Wilberforce* (Grand Rapids: Zondervan, 2007).
7. See Belmonte, *William Wilberforce*.
8. See Ronald Heifetz and Marty Linsky, *Leadership on the Line* (Boston: Harvard Business Review Press, 2002).
9. Patricia W. Linville, "Self-Complexity as a Cognitive Buffer Against Stress-Related Illness and Depression," *Journal of Personality and Social Psychology* 52, no. 4 (1987): 663–676.

10. Joshua Wolf Shenk, *Lincoln's Melancholy: How Depression Challenged a President and Fueled His Greatness* (New York: Mariner Books, 2006).

11. *The Diary of Orville Hickman Browning, Volume 1: 1850–1864*, ed. Theodore Calvin Pease and James G. Randall (Springfield: Illinois State Historical Library, 1925), p. 559.

12. Proverbs 17:22.

13. Alexander Wolfe, "Ellison Honors Jobs at Business Hall of Fame," *Forbes*, November 15, 2013, www.forbes.com/sites/oracle/2013/11/15/ellison-honors-steve-jobs-at-business-hall-of-fame/.

14. M. H. Abel, "Humor, Stress, and Coping Strategies," *Humor: International Journal of Humor Research* 15 (2002): 365–381.

15. Robert Mankoff, "Lincoln's Smile," *New Yorker* blog, November 28, 2012, www.newyorker.com/online/blogs/cartoonists/2012/11/lincolns-smile.html.

16. Cara MacInnis, "A Joke Is a Joke, Except When It Isn't," *Journal of Personality and Social Psychology* 99, no. 4 (2010): 660–682.

17. T. E. Ford, C. F. Boxer, J. Armstrong, and J. R. Edel, "More Than 'Just a Joke': The Prejudice-Releasing Function of Sexist Humor," *Personality and Social Psychology Bulletin* 34 (2008): 159–170; T. E. Ford and M. Ferguson, "Social Consequences of Disparagement Humor: A Prejudiced Norm Theory," *Personality and Social Psychology Review* 8 (2004): 79–94; T. E. Ford, E. R. Wentzel, and J. Lorion, "Effects of Exposure to Sexist Humor on Perceptions of Normative Tolerance of Sexism," *European Journal of Social Psychology* 31 (2001): 677–691.

18. Ford et al., "Effects of Exposure to Sexist Humor."

19. Arthur M. Nezu, Christine M. Nezu, Sonia E. Blissett, "Sense of Humor as a Moderator of the Relation Between Stressful Events and Psychological Distress: A Prospective Analysis," *Journal of Personality and Social Psychology* 54 (1988): 520–525.

20. Nezu et al., "Sense of Humor."

21. M. Söderström, K. Jeding, M. Ekstedt, A. Perski, and T. Aker-stedt, "Insufficient Sleep Predicts Clinical Burnout," *Journal of Occupational Health Psychology* 17, no. 2 (2012): 175–183.

22. Söderström et al., "Insufficient Sleep."

23. S. Sonnentag and U.-V. Bayer, "Switching Off Mentally: Predictors and Consequences of Psychological Detachment from Work During Off-Job Time," *Journal of Occupational Health Psychology* 10 (2005): 393–414.

24. Joshua Hammer, "Aung San Suu Kyi, Burma's Revolutionary Leader," *Smithsonian*, September 2012, www.smithsonianmag.com/people-places/Aung-San-Suu-Kyi-Burmas-Revolutionary-Leader-165590706.html#ixzz2DShqQLiT.

25. D. Etzion, D. Eden, and Y. Lapidot, "Relief from Job Stressors and Burnout: Reserve Service as a Respite," *Journal of Applied Psychology* 83 (1998): 577–585.

26. Mina Weston and Dov Eden, "Effects of Respite from Work on Burnout: Vacation Relief and Fade-out," *Journal of Applied Psychology* 82, no. 4 (1997): 516–527.

27. John Cooper, *Breaking the Heart of the World: Woodrow Wilson and the Fight for the League of Nations* (New York: Cambridge University Press, 2001).

28. Cooper, *Breaking the Heart of the World*, p. 111.

29. Cooper, *Breaking the Heart of the World*, p. 263.

30. Cooper, *Breaking the Heart of the World*, p. 189.

31. Cooper, *Breaking the Heart of the World*, p. 189.

Acknowledgments

I want to thank my wife, Rosie Lim, for the extraordinary partnership in writing this book and in my life. Her wisdom, perseverance, and talent contributed significantly to making the book a reality. It would not exist without her.

And thank you to the Berrett-Koehler team for the brilliant editorial and development support. In particular, I want to thank Steve Piersanti who worked with me every step on this demanding but joyous journey. What a privilege it has been to have him as my editor. And thank you to Laura Larson for reading the entire manuscript and providing detailed editing recommendations. She was very patient, extremely perceptive, and did an outstanding job.

Special thanks to my colleagues and partners in this leadership work: Ronnie Heifetz, Riley Sinder, Hugh O'Doherty, and Paul Porteous. What a team!

And thank you, Marie, Kristal, Shona, Chris, Kai, Addy, and Max. You have been my teachers and the source of my inspiration. Aloha.

Frank, June, Jon, and Cal have helped make my life exciting and abundant. I am so lucky and blessed by their spirits.

Index

Australia
  apology offered to Aboriginals in,
    155–156
  Zen slap of Gillard in, 88–89
Authority
  in big man leadership, 19, 21, 23
  of boundary keepers, 76
  compared to leadership, 10, 207n1
  dominance of, 130
  in Japanese culture, 16, 17
  self-reflection on, 170
  in transcending boundaries,
    130–131

B
Ba'ath Party, 73, 74, 211n20
Barra, Mary, 84
Barry, Marion, 69–70
Battle of Kosovo, 50–51
Beauty in play, 126
Begin, Menachem, 149
Bell, Genevieve, 116
Bell, Vanessa, 174
Bezos, Jeff, 30, 114
Biases, personal, self-reflection on,
    63, 64, 168–171
Big man leadership, 2, 4, 9–10,
    18–24
  of boundary keepers, 76
  of Gaddafi, 19–20
  at Lehman Brothers, 20–21
Black Harvest, 147
Blame
  in brittleness syndrome, 114
  in competing narratives, 138
  in failure or error, 114, 180
  in narrative of the other, 50–51
  self-reflection on, 180

Bogotá, Colombia, creative
    leadership of Mockus in,
    127–129
Bono, 25–26
Borneo, Penan of, 1–2
Boundaries, 2–3
  busting of, 5, 28, 81–109
  as constraint, 3, 5
  crossing of, 4–5, 27, 57–79
  diagnostic work on, 4, 33–53
  as frontier, 3, 140–142
  impact on company performance,
    13
  personal, expansion of, 5–6,
    165–183
  as protective barrier, 5, 12
  transcending of, 5, 28, 109–135
  and tribal impulse, 12
Boundary keepers
  in bridge-building work, 158
  in busting boundaries, 85, 99–102
  in crossing boundaries, 76–78
  grassroots movements in response
    to, 78, 99–102
  in transcending boundaries,
    130–132
Boutros-Ghali, Boutros, 136–137
Bremer, Paul, 72–73, 74, 211n17,
    211nn19–20
Bridge building between groups, 5,
    28, 135–161
  contact theory of, 142
  conversations in, 143–152
  crossing bridge in, 153–158
  descending ladder of
    interpretation in, 146–148
  discussing the undiscussable in,
    144–148, 217n9

About the Author

Dean Williams has been a faculty member at Harvard University's Kennedy School of Government since 1999 and is based at the Center for Public Leadership, where he directs the World Leaders Project. He is also the faculty chair of the executive education program, the Global Change Agent.

Dean served for five years as the chief adviser to the president of Madagascar, leading a comprehensive and innovative reform process for rapid development. He has also led major change processes, facilitated leadership development initiatives, and conducted research with governments, corporations, and educational systems in India, Australia, Nigeria, Singapore, Brunei, East Timor, Japan, Colombia, Cambodia, Europe, the Middle East, and the United States. He continues to work with businesses, governments, and institutions around the world on building leadership capacity to respond to the demands of leading in a crazy and fractured world.

Dean was born and raised in Australia. His first job was as a factory worker at Ford Motor Company. He later earned both master's and doctoral degrees from Harvard University, specializing in leadership and organizational development.

He is also the author of *Real Leadership: Helping People and Organizations Face Their Toughest Challenges.*

To learn more about Dean and his work, contact him here:

Website: www.GlobalLeadership.net

Email: dean@GlobalLeadership.net

Also by Dean Williams

Real Leadership
Helping People and Organizations Face Their Toughest Challenges

Much of what passes for "good leadership" today only appears effective because people are blindly following their leaders. But when organizations face tough challenges, leaders often offer false solutions and sidestep harsh realities, distracting people from the real work of progress. "Real leadership" mobilizes people to face reality and address the organization's or community's most pressing challenge—the primary threat or opportunity that must be confronted for success to unfold. The true task of a leader, Dean Williams argues, is to get people to face the reality of any situation *themselves*. Real leaders don't dictate; they help people face their challenges and make adjustments in their values, habits, practices, and priorities to ensure the enterprise is given its best chance to succeed. At a time when so many "visionary" leaders have led their organizations to disaster, *Real Leadership* offers a needed, proven alternative.

Hardcover, 312 pages, ISBN 978-1-57675-343-9
PDF ebook, ISBN 978-1-60509-618-6

Berrett–Koehler Publishers, Inc.
www.bkconnection.com

800.929.2929

Berrett–Koehler
Publishers

Berrett-Koehler is an independent publisher dedicated to an ambitious mission: *connecting people and ideas to create a world that works for all.*

We believe that to truly create a better world, action is needed at all levels—individual, organizational, and societal. At the individual level, our publications help people align their lives with their values and with their aspirations for a better world. At the organizational level, our publications promote progressive leadership and management practices, socially responsible approaches to business, and humane and effective organizations. At the societal level, our publications advance social and economic justice, shared prosperity, sustainability, and new solutions to national and global issues.

A major theme of our publications is "Opening Up New Space." Berrett-Koehler titles challenge conventional thinking, introduce new ideas, and foster positive change. Their common quest is changing the underlying beliefs, mindsets, institutions, and structures that keep generating the same cycles of problems, no matter who our leaders are or what improvement programs we adopt.

We strive to practice what we preach—to operate our publishing company in line with the ideas in our books. At the core of our approach is stewardship, which we define as a deep sense of responsibility to administer the company for the benefit of all of our "stakeholder" groups: authors, customers, employees, investors, service providers, and the communities and environment around us.

We are grateful to the thousands of readers, authors, and other friends of the company who consider themselves to be part of the "BK Community." We hope that you, too, will join us in our mission.

A BK Business Book

This book is part of our BK Business series. BK Business titles pioneer new and progressive leadership and management practices in all types of public, private, and nonprofit organizations. They promote socially responsible approaches to business, innovative organizational change methods, and more humane and effective organizations.

Berrett–Koehler
Publishers

Connecting people and ideas
to create a world that works for all

Dear Reader,

Thank you for picking up this book and joining our worldwide community of Berrett-Koehler readers. We share ideas that bring positive change into people's lives, organizations, and society.

To welcome you, we'd like to offer you a free e-book. You can pick from among twelve of our bestselling books by entering the promotional code **BKP92E** here: http://www.bkconnection.com/welcome.

When you claim your free e-book, we'll also send you a copy of our e-newsletter, the *BK Communiqué*. Although you're free to unsubscribe, there are many benefits to sticking around. In every issue of our newsletter you'll find

- A free e-book
- Tips from famous authors
- Discounts on spotlight titles
- Hilarious insider publishing news
- A chance to win a prize for answering a riddle

Best of all, our readers tell us, "Your newsletter is the only one I actually read." So claim your gift today, and please stay in touch!

Sincerely,

Charlotte Ashlock
Steward of the BK Website

Questions? Comments? Contact me at bkcommunity@bkpub.com.